I0814691

Rosemary
Lemon
Vinegar
TAAAAM
tape
teeth
slider
tab
stop
dots

YOUR COZY LIFE

DIY NESTING SKILLS FOR A SUSTAINABLE HOME

written and illustrated by

Raleigh Briggs

Microcosm Publishing

Portland, OR

Your Cozy Life: DIY Nesting Skills for a Sustainable Home
© Raleigh Briggs, 2025
This edition © Microcosm Publishing, 2025
This is Microcosm #956
ISBN 9781648414831
Originally published as *Make Your Place* (2007), *How to Make Soap (without burning your face off)* (2011), and *Make It Last* (2012)
First Edition, originally published March, 2025
Cover and Book Design by Joe Biel

Microcosm Publishing
2752 N Williams Ave
Portland, OR 97227
(503)799-2698
Write or visit for a catalog
All the news that's fit to print at www.Microcosm.Pub/Newsletter

Get more from the author at www.Microcosm.Pub/Raleigh

Find more books like this at www.Microcosm.pub/GoodLife

To join the ranks of high-class stores that feature Microcosm titles, talk to your rep: In the U.S. **COMO** (Atlantic), **ABRAHAM** (Midwest), **BOB BARNETT** (Texas, Oklahoma, Arkansas, Louisiana), **IMPRINT** (Pacific), **TURNAROUND** (UK), **UTP/MANDA** (Canada), **NEWSOUTH** (Australia/New Zealand), **Observatoire** (Africa, Europe), **IPR** (Middle East), **Yvonne Chau** (Southeast Asia), **HarperCollins** (India), **Everest/B.K. Agency** (China), **Tim Burland** (Japan/Korea), and **FAIRE** in the gift trade.

EU Safety Information: https://microcosmpublishing.com/gpsr

Global labor conditions are bad, and our roots in industrial Cleveland in the 70s and 80s made us appreciate the need to treat workers right. Therefore, our books are MADE IN THE USA.

MICROCOSM PUBLISHING is Portland's most diversified publishing house and distributor, with a focus on the colorful, authentic, and empowering. Our books and zines have put your power in your hands since 1996, equipping readers to make positive changes in their lives and in the world around them. Microcosm emphasizes skill-building, showing hidden histories, and fostering creativity through challenging conventional publishing wisdom with books and bookettes about DIY skills, food, bicycling, gender, self-care, and social justice. What was once a distro and record label started by Joe Biel in a drafty bedroom was determined to be *Publishers Weekly*'s fastest-growing publisher of 2022 and #3 in 2023 and 2024, and is now among the oldest independent publishing houses in Portland, OR, and Cleveland, OH. In 2024, Biel won the PubWest Innovator Award. Microcosm remains a politically moderate, centrist publisher in a world that has inched to the right for the past 80 years.

Did you know that you can buy our books directly from us at sliding scale rates? Support a small, independent publisher and pay less than Amazon's price at **www.Microcosm.Pub**.

I have people to thank! Give it up for: Lacey Clemmons, Corinne Manning + Kathryn Higgins for their editorial guidance; Kim Reinauer for her canning expertise; ZAPP and its volunteers, both past and present; the Seattle Public Library, as usual; and my man Greg Brown, as always.

introduction

Hello, my sweet friends.

Thank you for picking up this special omnibus, Your Cozy Life! If you had told me fifteen years ago that the humble zines I'd scribbled down would become books that are still finding new readers, I would not have believed you. What a trip! And what an honor to be on your shelf and in your life. Connecting to so many people through this work feels both cozy and expansive, like snuggling under a blanket to watch the stars. * *

I hope these pages bring you comfort and inspiration. I hope they help you connect with your community and build networks of care in the real, touchable, unmemeable world.

Thank you so much for all your love and support. I appreciate it so much. ♡

Love always,

♡ raleigh ♡

♡ ♡

Rosemary
Lemon
Vinegar
stop
tape
teeth
slider
tab

TABLE OF CONTENTS

make
your
place
written + illustrated
by Raleigh Briggs

Introduction

When Make Your Place was first published, I always had to hunt for it in bookstores. (Yes, I look for my own books. I am complicated and imperfect.) It is a stubborn, genre-resisting book, and it must have been a pain for booksellers to shelve. Sometimes I'd discover it looking small and scrappy next to the glossy self-help books; sometimes it would be nestled like a sprout amongst the cookbooks or gardening manuals. How times have changed! Today, there are whole shelves of DIY books, and the Internet is lousy with clever "hacks" for things even I would never think to make myself.

And yet, my little sprout-book is still here, and still in print. To this day I get emails from all over the world. I go to new friends' houses for the first time, only to find a copy of Make Your Place on their shelf. Even with hundreds of titles to choose from, people continue to connect with my short, weirdly spaced, handwritten book. ♡ I am utterly humbled and deeply honored. ♡

But of course, I didn't invent this. I am just a conduit. Every bit of knowledge in the DIY world (and in this book) was passed down from folks who, because of their class, race, or gender, had to find a way to survive without the privilege of money and resources. We must honor that. This has been on my mind a lot in the ten years (WHAT) that this book has been in the world: how important it is to celebrate the ingenuity of DIY while being critical of the system that made it necessary in the first place. I hope you'll read with that intent, whether you're new to this book or just revisiting it.

It can be beautiful and freeing to create a life for yourself with your own hands, but we cannot stop there. How can we use these skills to build each other up? How can we extend that beauty and freedom to everyone, whether they share our privileges or not?*

*And especially if they don't!

That's my dream for the next leg of this little book's journey. Because if DIY frees us, it's gotta free all of us.

Thank you so, so much for reading. I hope you enjoy. ♡

Much love and gratitude,

(Raleigh Briggs, Seattle, August 2017)

Note the zine archive where this book was conceived, Seattle's Zine Archive and Publishing Project (ZAPP), has gone to the great free copy shop in the sky. Its absence has left a sizable hole in my heart. So I dedicate this book to the decades of ZAPP coordinators, volunteers, and patrons: you made that place, that mad scientist's lab of dreams and ideas, my very first home in my adopted city. None of this would have been written without you.

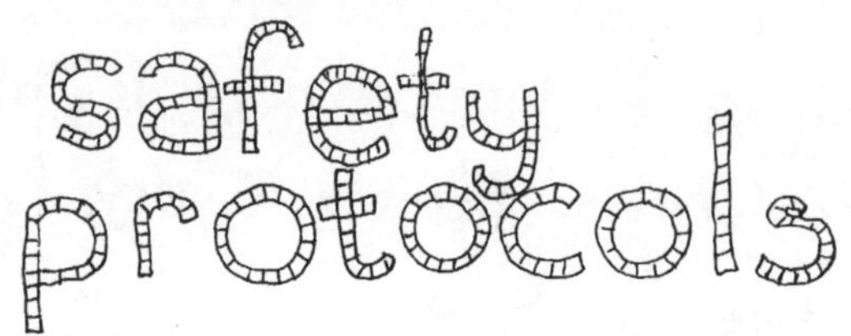

In this book, I've tried my best to include only recipes made with safe or safeish ingredients; however, like your favorite animal, even natural formulas can hurt you if you disrespect them. That said, here are some things to keep in mind:

Protocol 1: Natural ≠ Edible

Even though compounds like borax and washing soda are far safer than most of the ingredients you'll find lurking in your local drugstore, they shouldn't accidentally get inside your body. Same goes for essential oils, which are far too potent to use internally. Wash your hands after mixing cleaners and label the containers you keep them in. If you have sensitive skin, wear gloves when you clean.

Protocol 2: Wildcraft with Care

I am confident that everyone reading this knows not to carelessly pull plants out of the ground and eat them. Still, it bears repeating that if you wildcraft food and herbs, you need to do your research. A lot of communities offer free or low-cost wildcrafting workshops. Check out local parks departments, agricultural nonprofits, community colleges, and punk houses or co-ops. At the very least, get yourself a full-color field guide with large photos, and when you do find something foragable, collect it in a respectful and responsible way.

Protocol 3: Think of the Unborn Children!

If you're pregnant, please avoid the following essential oils and herbs:

clary sage	calendula	sage
juniper	camphor	St. John's Wort
cinnamon	comfrey	thyme
cedarwood	lemon balm	wintergreen
clove	neem	basil
anise	pennyroyal	myrrh

Protocol 4: Know Your Body

This, I think, is most important: if something makes you feel gross, or itchy, or you'd really rather take a pill, listen to your gut and do what is best for your terrifically free and unique body. This book is about making your life better, not about being hardcore.

Protocol 5: Plants Have Families

You know that botanical horror called ragweed? It's related to both calendula and chamomile. So if you have a ragweed allergy, avoid using any herb related to ragweed for cosmetic or medicinal purposes. Sorry.

chapter 1

Health + First Aid

★ and now, a short musing on health ★

Whenever I get into conversations about DIY I find that certain ideas get echoed by many different people. Chief among these tenets is the idea that DIY is about making even the tiny bits of our lives intentional: we focus our energy on what we know is right for us, rather than what is dictated by a market or culture. I think herbal medicine and DIY healthcare are such a strong manifestation of this idea. There is definitely a place for conventional medicine - it saves lives, after all. It's quick and effective and familiar. But it has the unfortunate effect of distancing us from our bodies. Instead of questioning why we have constant digestive issues, for example, we end up just tossing pills down our gullets like we're balancing the pH of a swimming pool. It's cold and isolating, not to mention expensive.

Compare this to the practice of using herbs, which work in a broader, less symptom-focused way. In the DIY healthcare mindset, you would tone a weak GI tract and strengthen it, rather than dulling it with antispasmodics. Natural medicine often takes time, but within that time there is an invitation to actually witness your body changing. It forces you to pay attention to the systems of your body, and how they interact and signal each other. Over time, we become less afraid of our mysterious guts and tunnels, and thus, more confident in our ability to heal ourselves. And that's what this chapter is all about!

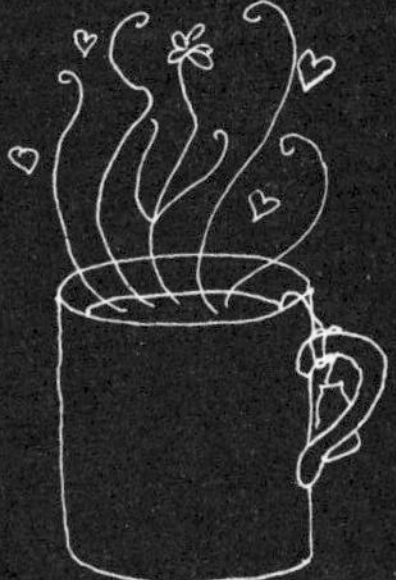

a Quick Guide to Essential Oils

Always use pure essential oil when you're making cleaners or remedies. Don't use anything labeled "perfume oil" or "aromatherapy oil." Essential oils can retain some of the antimicrobial, antibacterial, and antiviral properties of the whole plant. These oils are highly concentrated and volatile, so keep them in dark glass bottles away from direct sunlight and heat. And DO NOT EAT THEM.!

Here are some oils that come in handy:

• Antibacterial: bay, camphor, cardamom, chamomile, citronella, cypress, eucalyptus, ginger, hyssop, juniper, lavender, lemon, lemongrass, lemon verbena, lime, marjoram, orange, pine, rosemary, sage, sandalwood, spearmint, tea tree, thyme

• Antimicrobial: bergamot, chamomile, clove, eucalyptus, hyssop, lavender, lemon, lime, myrtle, nutmeg, oregano, patchouli, tea tree

• Antiviral: cinnamon, eucalyptus, lavender, lemon, oregano, sandalwood, tea tree, thyme

*NOTE: Please please please read the section on Safety before you use oils. It's important to me.

How-tos - basic recipes for salves, tinctures, and sundry curiousities

The following recipes are a good starting point for any budding (har!) herbalist. One small note: if you have the funds and the space available, I would recommend keeping a set of cooking tools exclusively for the purpose of making herbal remedies. Ideally this will include:

- an enamel or stainless steel pan, double boiler, or slow cooker
- a funnel
- cheesecloth or coffee filters
- a mortar + pestle (...or a plastic bag and a trusty cudgel)
- dark glass jars and bottles - use the kind with droppers if you are making tinctures, and fatter, wider jars with twisty lids for salves
- larger glass jars (jam + pickle jars are excellent) with tight-fitting lids, for steeping and soaking herbs
- a stirring utensil

making tinctures

A tincture is basically a combination of an herb and an appropriate solvent that is allowed to steep for several weeks. The result is a highly concentrated solution that captures the healing properties of the plant.

Tinctures are awesome because they're easy to make, portable, and if you make and store them properly, they'll stay potent for quite a while. They can be used to soak gauze for compresses, combined with creams or oils, or taken internally at a ratio of 30 or so drops in one glass of water, juice or tea.

To make a tincture, chop up a cup of whatever herb or herbs you are using (roots or woody stems should be dried and ground in a mortar and pestle). It is very important that you use dried herbs when you make salves + tinctures — the water in fresh herbs can harbor bacteria that will ruin your work. (Either lay herbs flat to dry or tie into small bundles and hang somewhere dry and sunny. To rig up a quick herb drying rack, secure herbs to a metal coathanger with some clothespins, and hang near a window or radiator)

Take your chopped herbs or roots and place them in a clean jar with a tight-fitting lid – a pickle or mayonnaise jar works great, just make sure it's a big'un. Cover the herbs with 5 cups of cheap 60 proof vodka; for a non-alcoholic version with some added health benefits, use apple cider vinegar. Seal up your jar and hide it from your friends in a cool, dark place. Let it sit there for two weeks, and give it a good shake every once in a while. When the two weeks are up, line a funnel

see? – with several layers of cheese-cloth and strain the tincture into dark glass bottles. Pull the corners of the cheesecloth into a nice package and squeeze out any liquid before tossing the solids.

fig. A

Cap your tinctures tightly, make some cute labels for them and keep them away from heat and light.

Ta DAH!

making infusions, decoctions + poultices

An infusion is a quantity of water or other liquid in which herbs have been steeped long enough for the properties of the herbs to transfer to the water. Usually, the water is first boiled, and then poured over the plant matter. Yes, this is pretty much the same thing as tea; in fact, I will use the words "tea" and "infusion" interchangeably in this book. To make an infusion, boil one cup of water for every teaspoon or so of dried leaves, soft stems, or flowers (we'll get to bark + roots in a second). If you're using fresh herbs, make sure to wash them well, and double the amount you're using. Pour the boiling water down over the herbs, cover and let steep until cool. The best way to do this is in a mason jar. For stronger infusions, use more herbs or let the jar sit for longer. When steepage is complete, strain out all the plant material, transfer to a clean jar, and refrigerate what you don't use right away.

Decoctions are a lot like infusions, but making them involves boiling the herbs and water together. This method is used for woody stems, bark and roots. Combine 1 oz herb with a quart of water and boil, covered, for 20 minutes. From there, follow the instructions for making infusions.

A poultice is basically a pulp made of herbs, and sometimes other ingredients, that is applied directly to the skin to treat swelling, bites, and so on. To make a poultice, grind fresh herbs until juicy and/or sticky. If you're dealing with dryish plants, moisten the mixture with a little clean water, or better yet, an herbal infusion or decoction.

Infused oils can be used for massage, skin and hair care. Bruise a handful of fresh herbs by rolling them between your hands, and stick them in an airtight bottle filled with your favorite carrier oil. I like almond, grapeseed, and cheap (not extra virgin) olive oils. Cap the bottle tightly and keep it in a cool, dark place, like a kitchen cupboard. Shake it once and a while and strain out the herbs after a week or so.

making salves

Salves seem intimidating, but they are surprisingly easy to make, and they're pretty impressive when they're finished. Salves protect and nourish the skin while it's healing. You can make salves by stewing herbs in oil and adding beeswax as a thickener and skin protectant. You can also use infused oils you've already made. For equipment, you'll need an enamel or glass pot, a wooden spoon, and a grater.

Salve A: Infused-Oil Method

2 oz infused oil
2 T grated beeswax
2 drops essential oil (optional)

Warm the oil over low heat until just hot. Add the beeswax and stir the mixture until all the wax is melted. Add the oil if you're using it.

Pour the mixture into a small glass jar and let it cool. At this point it should be solid. If it's too solid, reheat the salve and add another drizzle of oil. If it's too soft, reheat and add more wax. When it's the right consistency, pour it back into the little jar, cap it tightly, and label it.

Salve B: Stewed-Herb Method

2 oz dried herbs

1 cup (8 fl. oz) olive oil

1 oz beeswax (will vary according to how soft you want your salve to be), grated

Place the herbs and oil in an enamel pot, bring to a low heat (*not a boil*) and stew the herbs until the oil is dark green with herby juices (up to 3 hours) Stir occasionally. Strain out the herbs through two layers of cheese-cloth and return the oil to the pot. Add the beeswax and stir until totally melted. Pour the salve into wee jars and let cool.

Variation: After the salve is cooked, beat it for a minute or so with an electric mixer or an egg beater, to make a creamier salve.

You can also try stewing your herbs and oil in a slow cooker set to low, for 8-10 hours.

Vegan Alternatives to Beeswax include soy wax, carnauba wax and candellilia wax. You'll have to experiment with the proportions of wax to oil, as these waxes behave differently than bees-wax. Carnauba wax, for example, is much harder. You might also try melting some virgin coconut oil, which is solid at room temperature, and infusing it, then letting it resolidify. Keep the oil in a cool, dark place, especially in the summer.

anatomy of an herbal first aid kit

Here are some basic remedies and hardware to stock in a good first aid kit. This is a big list, so feel free to tailor it to your lifestyle. For example, if you spend a lot of time outdoors, pack a poison ivy remedy and some aloe vera, and cut back on tinctures for headaches, etc.

ALLOVER HEALTH TONICS

...because some herbs are so great you'll want to take them every day.

Burdock root is used as a vegetable in Japan. It's also a great tonic for the liver, skin, bladder, and blood. The fuzzy burrs of the burdock plant are the inspiration for velcro! To use burdock, make a decoction with the root, or chew a fresh hunk of root.

It sucks that nettles are so jabby and despised, because they're actually AWESOME. Nettles are high in protein, iron, and vitamins. You can buy dried nettles and make tea, but you can also wildcraft them and eat them like spinach. To pick nettles, wear gloves, strip off young, tender leaves, and boil, steam or sauté them to get rid of those stingers!

Astragalus root is an immune system tonic that's especially important in traditional Chinese medicine. Like Echinacea, it's popular during cold + flu season. You can take astragalus on its own, but most prefer to combine it with other herbs they like, such as nettles or chamomile.

Damiana is a small Central American shrub that smells kind of like chamomile. Why do you care? Because it's an aphrodisiac! GO FOR IT!!

CUTS + SCRAPES

Firstly, some friendly advice: the following remedies are really for mild cuts, scrapes + irritations. If you gash yourself up really good please do not pour cayenne in it. It will suck. Anyway:

• Use the aforementioned cayenne, in powder form, as a styptic – aka a blood-clotting agent. Sprinkle a little right on the cut or scrape. It does smart a bit, though – you can also use comfrey or yarrow.

• Tea tree oil is a powerful antimicrobial agent. Dilute several drops of tea tree oil in a couple tablespoons of oil (almond or grapeseed oil is nice, but olive or vegetable oil works fine too) and apply to cuts, abrasions, fungal infections and skin irritations.

• Whip up an all-purpose healing salve for your various injuries and skin problems. Some good herbs to use for their soothing, antiseptic, and painkilling properties: comfrey, calendula, meadowsweet, goldenseal, marshmallow and horsebalm. Direct your attention to page 14 for instructions for making salves.

* NOTE: You can also make a tincture with any or all of the above herbs and apply to the skin as a wet compress with a dry bandage on top. *

Aches & Sprains

Arnica is a lovely, yellow-bloomed member of the sunflower family that has been used for centuries to treat sprains, bruises, and muscle aches. While you should not take arnica internally, feel free to distill it into a tincture, use the flower heads in a salve, or mash them up and apply as a poultice to a sprained ankle. A quick compress for bruises and swelling can be made by soaking some clean gauze with arnica tincture and applying it to your (unbroken) skin. If you have sensitive skin or allergies, dilute the tincture with water, or use arnica infusion.

Arnica flowers also work well as part of a blend: for an excellent muscle salve, use equal parts arnica, witch hazel, and St. John's Wort. This formula is nice, because unlike a lot of commercial formulas that are supermentholated, it soothes your muscles without making you feel like your skin is on fire. But if you like that feeling, turn the page!

For a headier-smelling concoction with a bit of a tingle to it, combine an appropriate carrier oil (more on that in a minute) with a couple drops each of camphor, eucalyptus, rosemary, and clove bud oils. These essential oils are cooling and antiseptic; camphor and clove also have mild analgesic properties when applied topically. Shake your new massage oil well and rub into sore or tired muscles.

When you're making oils for your skin, it's important to choose an oil with the right consistency for your intended purpose, and one that's not too greasy. For massage, almond oil is always nice, and grapeseed oil is a good alternative for oilier skin. You can also try coconut oil — coconut oil is great for the skin, and is solid at room temperature, making it more portable. Just be sure it's melted when you mix in your essential oils. You can do this by placing your jar of oil in a big bowl of very hot water.

NOTE: Even though it's cheap, resist the temptation of mineral oil (baby oil). That "mineral" is petroleum, and that's what the oil feels like: gross, gloppy, and pore-clogging as all get out. Nast.

Burns, Rashes and skin conditions

Ahem: the following remedies work great for mild burns and sunburns. If you've burnt a large area of your body, or you've got chemical or electric burns, *for the love of God go to the ER.* And I hope you're okay.

Anyway, so you've burned yourself: your first course of action should be to cool your burnt skin under a cold tap or in an ice bath. Immediate cold will help prevent further injury, and in those first moments it will lessen your pain a great deal. While you're sitting there, drink a glass or two of cool water. Dehydration is a serious side effect of burns and sunburns, and not a lot of people realize how quickly it can set in.

DO! NOT! PUT GREASE! ON A BURN! That includes stuff like butter and petroleum jelly. Any oil will effectively trap heat against your skin, which is really the last thing you want. An oil barrier will also hinder air circulation and proper drainage, both of which are crucial to healing.

Now I am contractually obligated to talk about aloe vera. Just kidding! I will blab about aloe willingly, earnestly, joyfully. It really is the best thing to use on any type of burn. On top of that, aloe is easy to grow and process yourself. To make DIY aloe gel, puree a couple handfuls of peeled aloe leaves with 150 IU of Vitamin C powder. Vitamin C is a natural preservative like Vitamin E and jojoba oil —but without the oil. Store your gel in the fridge - it keeps longer and feels nicer that way.

Other herbs that are good for burns include calendula, comfrey, chamomile, St. John's wort and plantain. If you have the essential oils of any of these plants, mix a few drops with some aloe gel (homemade, of course). Alternately, make a strong infusion with any or all of the above herbs, let it cool completely, and either apply as a compress or add to a cool bath. Whatever you do, <u>don't</u> use tinctures on burns. Tinctures are drying, and if you put them on burnt skin, it feels like you're soaking a hangnail in acetone - oh man, it hurts so bad. So don't do it!

For other skin ailments, like eczema and dermatitis, calendula and marshmallow are always good options. Either stew the herbs into a salve, use their infusions as a body splash or bath additive, or add a couple dropperfuls of tincture to some natural, unscented hand cream. Soap made with calendula petals is also nice.

Poison Ivy, Nettle, Etc.

A lot of folks swear by the inner flesh of the spotted jewelweed plant as a remedy for poison ivy. Jewelweed grows rampant all over the East Coast of North America. Look for it growing in wet environments, like creek beds. To use it, grab a stem and split it open. Rub the juicy inside of the stem over your rash.

For those of us in the West and beyond, plantain (the herb, not the fruit) is an excellent alternative. Different species of plantain grow all over the world, and many of these thrive as weeds in urban areas. To calm itching and pain associated with stings, rashes and skin

Calendula

irritations, crush or chew fresh plantain leaf and stick the resulting cud on the affected area.

basic healing poultice powder

This is a basic formula for an all-purpose skin powder. It's good for blistered feet, small cuts, and when mixed with water to form a paste, is very soothing to rashes and insect bites...

1 part dried plantain
1 part goldenseal root
1 part dried marshmallow
1 part dried calendula

Grind everything into a fine powder using a coffee grinder, and keep in a plastic zip-top bag.

...and speaking of bug bites!

Tinctures of witch hazel, plantain, grindelia, comfrey, and St. John's wort are itch relievers. Add some to a bit of oil or lotion for a lone bite, or add diluted tincture (or infusion) to your bathwater. Lavender oil, diluted in a bit of almond oil, is also good for bites. And while you're in the tub, throw in a handful of baking soda, another great bite remedy.

To repel bugs, combine one, some, or all of the following essential oils in a base of vegetable oil (or equal parts vodka and water), and store in a spray bottle. Don't use more than 20 or so drops of essential oil altogether:

★ lavender ★ citronella ★ eucalyptus ★ cedarwood ★ lemongrass ★

Bite + Sting Plaster

This is like a tiny face mask for your bug bites. It's especially good for treating stings from bees, wasps, and yellow jackets.

1 part tincture of plantain (you can also use echinacea or comfrey)
1 part pure water (distilled)
1 part kaolin or bentonite clay (an astri-ngent clay that is usually available in bulk at co-ops and via mail order)
A few drops of lavender essential oil (max 3)

Mix the ingredients together in a small bowl. Tweak the dry-to-wet ratio until the resulting paste is smooth and tacky enough to adhere to your skin. Mound a small bit of plaster on top of the bite and let it dry, at which point you can wash or rub it off.

This plaster will keep in an airtight container, but only for a little while. Try making a batch right before a picnic/hayride/kid's birthday party or other bug-friendly event.

Bruises, Bleeding, and other "Sports Injuries"

Arnica and comfrey are the first herbs you should reach for when you've got a bruise. Start by making an infusion of one or both plants and letting it cool. Then, either use the tea as a wet compress, or freeze it in ice cube trays, wrap the ice in a tea towel and apply to the bruise (don't use a plastic bag—you want the tea to wash over the bruise as it melts). The ice method is preferred whenever the bruise is accompanied by swelling.

Nosebleeds

If your nose bleeds often, keep on hand a bottle of yarrow tincture. Yarrow is a natural styptic and will help stop bleeding. Fold a length of clean fabric until it fits over the bridge of your nose, soak it in a combination of one teaspoon yarrow tincture and one cup water, and press the compress firmly over your nose. Lean forward and let your head rest between your knees. Try to relax and breathe deeply through your mouth. Make another compress with the yarrow tincture and place it across the back of your neck. With your free hand apply pressure to your upper lip.

PARASITES

If you've ever had head lice, you know that the treatment is this vile, burning shampoo that is just as awful as having lice. Essential oil of thyme is an effective herbal alternative because thyme is very high in phenol, an antiseptic and anti-parasitic chemical compound that's also present in other plants, like tea tree. To treat lice, add four drops of thyme oil in an ounce or two of olive oil and rub it in to your scalp. Put on a shower cap and relax for a half hour. Wash your hair with soap or shampoo and then comb the nits (tiny lice eggs) out with a very fine-toothed nit comb. Make sure you get every last nit - they look like little white dots clinging to your hair shaft. In the meantime, wash your sheets in the hottest water you can procure, and add some thyme oil to your laundry soap Oh yeah - you can treat crabs this way too.

Thyme

*CAUTION: IF YOU ARE PREGNANT, DON'T USE THYME - JUST SHAVE YOUR HEAD

the fungus among us

Fungal infections can occur in several different areas of the body: athlete's foot, jock itch, ringworm, yeast infections and thrush are all types of fungal infection. They all suck pretty bad. Fortunately, most are quite easy to treat.

The first thing you should do to fight off a fungus is to increase the friendly bacteria in your body by taking some probiotics. These are found naturally in cultured products like yogurt and kefir (look for "active" or "live cultures" on the label), but you can find extracted probiotics like acidophilus in pill form too. For yeast infections, use yogurt (*plain* yogurt) topically in and around your genitals – use a little spoon or a tampon applicator to get it in there. Wear a pad afterwards while the yogurt's leaking out. Another remedy is to wrap a peeled clove of garlic in some cheesecloth, dip it in olive oil and insert it into the vagina You can tie a string around it for easy removal. Change the clove 3 times a day. If you'd rather avoid putting stuff inside you, or if you don't have a vagina, eating lots of yogurt and garlic can also be effective.

External infections, like athlete's foot, can be treated with antifungal herbs like tea tree oil. Here's a simple ointment that you can use all over:

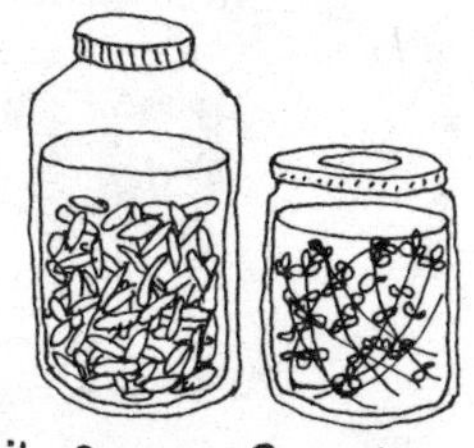

1 cup olive oil
big handful calendula petals
10 drops tea tree oil

Infuse the calendula in the oil for a few days, then add the tea tree oil. Keep the ointment in a tight-lidded jar. Use as a massage oil on the infected area a couple times a day. If you have dandruff or a scalp infection, rub the ointment into your scalp, pull on a kerchief or shower cap, and sleep on it. Wash the oil out in the morning.

Antiseptic + Antifungal Soap

Use this on your hair and body

8 oz liquid castile soap, unscented
10 drops tea tree oil
5 drops lavender essential oil
5 drops eucalyptus essential oil

Add the oils to the soap and mix well. Store in a squeeze bottle.

More tricks:

- For especially itchy infections, like yeast infections, try soaking in a bath with a few handfuls of baking soda tossed in.
- Paint gentian violet tincture on any fungal infection. For yeast, soak a tampon in the solution. Make sure to wear a pad, because the stuff is purple.
- If your feet burn and itch, get someone to rub them with aloe vera gel with a couple drops of tea tree oil added in.

Digestive issues can be either acute or chronic, and they are always pretty sucky. Fortunately, there are herbs out there that can work as digestive tonics that strengthen your GI tract, which makes it easier for you to manage a chronic condition. Among these, the most accessible is chamomile. Awesome, right? Because you already *like* chamomile! A strong cup of chamomile tea, taken three times a day, can tone a weak set of guts over time. Soothing.

For digestive complaints, I always prefer teas to tinctures, which are alcohol-based and can irritate an uppity stomach. If you've got the runs, check out raspberry leaf, blackberry leaf, slippery elm, and cranesbill. Let your herbs steep 10-30 minutes and drink a few cups, or until you're feeling better. In the meantime, make yourself a bowl of cooked white rice, avoid any foods that you know irritate your stomach, and make sure to drink lots of water to counteract dehydration.

If you just barely ate something really gross and a cold dread is creeping up your esophagus, reach for some charcoal tablets — tablets, <u>not</u> briquettes! The charcoal is incredibly absorbant and will help to soak up your warm mayonnaise or whatever the hell that was. Follow the directions on the bottle, or take one or two tablets every four hours.

UGH

BARF!

For nausea + motion sickness, try ginger, everyone's favorite rhizome. You can buy ginger powdered in tablets, but candied ginger is much tastier. You can buy it in bulk at most co-ops, health food stores, and Asian groceries.

Herbal teas are also helpful if you're backed up — try yellow dock, milk thistle, senna, and cascara sagrada. A cup of yerba maté tea, taken on an empty stomach, can also speed things up.* In between cups of tea, stick to a diet nigh in fiber, and try to move around a little. And yes, prunes will help you — a *lot*.

PLUHHHM

* Avoid this if you're sensitive to caffeine, or have ulcers

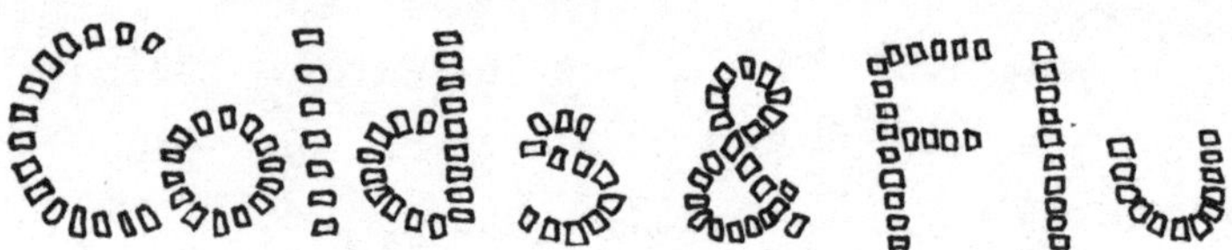

There are so many herbs that fight colds, I'm just going to list them:

- Echinacea
- Boneset
- Goldenseal
- Garlic
- Usnea

Antimicrobial herbs that work to kill infections in the body and support the immune system

- Valerian
- Cramp Bark
- Passionflower

Antispasmodics, for cramps and body aches

- Meadowsweet
- Slippery Elm
- Raspberry Leaf

Help reduce mucus secretions

- Elder Flower
- Peppermint
- Yarrow

Herbs that induce sweating, for reducing fevers

- Comfrey
- Coltsfoot
- Mullein
- Marshmallow
- Licorice

Expectorants, to help you cough it up

- Catnip
- Hops

Mild sedatives, for better rest

*I recommend making a big thermosful of tea using a few of these herbs. Keep it next to your bed so you don't have to keep getting up to make tea. This also helps you to stay hydrated. Here's a good general cold/flu formula:

Cold & Flu Tea

1/4 c each:
Elder flowers
Licorice
Boneset

1/8 c Meadowsweet

1/8 c Catnip

2 T each:
Peppermint
Cramp Bark

Store in an airtight jar. Use one tablespoon herbs for every cup of water.

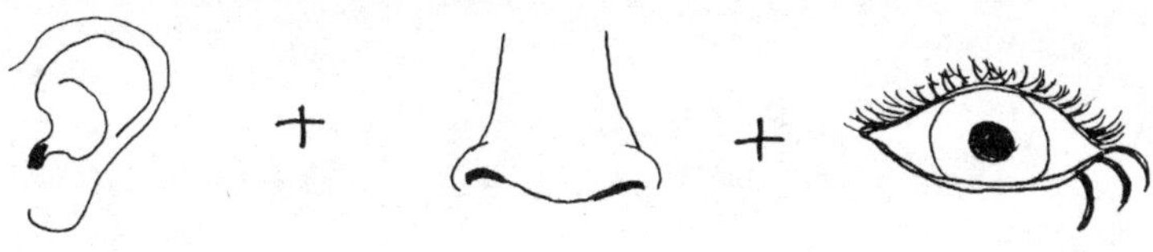

Mullein Ear Oil

Mullein is an anti-inflammatory, and a traditional herb for earaches.

• Combine in a small jar a handful of dried mullein flowers and a clove of sliced garlic (optional). Cover the herbs with olive oil, cap the jar, and let it sit in a sunny spot for a few days. Strain out the flowers and transfer the oil to a dropper bottle. Use 2-3 drops in your achey ear once or twice a day. Warm it up first if you like - just stick it in your pocket for a minute.

Sinus Wash

One of the simplest ways to treat congestion is to irrigate your sinuses with a saline solution. Use a neti pot or a cup to pour this mixture gently into one nostril and let it drip out the other. Refill the pot and repeat on the other side, and then gently blow your nose. Use 1/8 t sea salt to every cup of warm water, and add a pinch of baking soda.

Herbal Eye Wash

Eyebright. Guess what it does!

Make an infusion with one cup of water plus 1/2 teaspoon each:

eyebright
goldenseal root
red raspberry leaf

Strain it <u>very</u> well and use it with an eye cup or shot glass to help soothe tired eyes or fight eye infections.

mouth & tooth issues

Oil of clove is an important ingredient in a lot of dental products, including crowns (if you've ever had a root canal: oil of clove is why your crown sometimes smells improbably like perfume). Clove oil has strong antiseptic and painkilling properties, and can be found in most drugstores, in the pharmacy section next to the other "olde tyme apothecary" stuff. Put a drop on a cotton swab or bit of dental floss, and apply to your aching tooth, making sure not to swallow any.

Thyme is another herb with a stellar reputation for killin' germs. You can use a strong tea or diluted thyme tincture as a mouth rinse to clean mouth wounds and lessen your chances of infection.

If you are completely bereft of all healing plants, make a solution of warm water and sea salt. Sea salt is naturally astringent and is perfect for gently cleansing tissue that's healing from trauma. Sea salt solution works to temporarily soothe sore throats, also.

I've always had the kind of blitzkrieg PMS that seems to assault every organ in my body at the same time. Maybe you also have this problem. To counteract a number of different symptoms, make a tea blend with the following and drink 2-3 cups a day:

- 2 T dandelion root — diuretic to help swelling and/or bloating. Also full of iron + nutrients
- 2 T chamomile
- 2 T lemon balm — (chamomile and lemon balm:) calming, for emotional support
- 2 t raspberry leaf
- 2 t cramp bark — (raspberry leaf and cramp bark:) antispasmodics to soothe cramps
- 2 t fresh ginger — aids digestion and is tasty

Valerian is also excellent for stopping cramps—since it's also a sedative, it's best used to treat nighttime cramps, or cramps you have when you know you aren't going to do anything productive. You can also take cramp bark tincture, which is quite effective.

If you're bloated and uncomfortable, make sure to drink lots of water and herbal tea. If you can find young dandelion greens to eat, they are super nutritious and will help flush out retained fluid. Avoid coffee- even though it makes you pee, it doesn't help with water retention. Ain't that a kick in the ass?

If you have ongoing menstrual troubles like erratic periods, painful periods or especially heavy bleeding, try drinking red raspberry leaf tea as a uterine tonic. Drink a cup or two a day, and add an extra cup when you're menstruating, to help with cramps.

Emmenagogues are herbs that stimulate menstruation —which, by the way, is different than inducing miscarriage or abortion.* Emmenagogues are what you use if your period is just being pokey because you're stressed, overworked, underweight, or you have a hormonal or metabolic imbalance.

Parsley is a well-known emmenagogue, and is super-nutritious and tasty. Take parsley as an infusion, 2-3 times a day, or eat fresh parsley salads, until your period comes. Other emmenagogues include ginger, yarrow, sage, rosemary, blue cohosh root, and motherwort. You can take these herbs as infusions, 1-3 times a day, for up to a week. Don't use these if you're pregnant.

If your flow is super heavy, try tinctures of yarrow, vitex berry, and red raspberry leaf. Up your intake of iron until you feel better.

* NOTE: I made an executive decision not to cover herbal contraception + abortion in this book — not because I have anything against it, but because I have no experience with it at all. If you need resources on this, check out the amazing women's health zines on page 123.

HEADACHES

Headaches get their own section in this chapter because they are such vicious, elusive little buggers. As anyone who has dealt with chronic headaches knows, painkillers - even herbal ones - are often not enough to solve the problem, because your headache may very well be a mere symptom of a larger problem, like:

- bacterial infection
- allergies
- poor vision
- PMS
- stress
- and more!

But I'm not trying to freak you out. If one of the herbal pain relief tinctures on page 40 doesn't work for you, you're most likely stressed out or dehydrated. If you find yourself in this situation often, try some basic aromatherapy. The essential oils of lavender, peppermint, and chamomile are well-known stress relievers. If you keep a bottle of this blend around, you'll find it useful in all sorts of formulas. Try mixing a few drops with unscented soap or lotion and massage your neck and temples. Or just keep it around and inhale the scent when you're feeling stressed.

You can also use your new blend in an herbal eye pillow. Cut a square of soft fabric into an 8 × 8 swatch and fold it in half with the right sides facing in. Using a tight stitch, sew up one short side and one long side. Turn the pouch inside out.

① 8" 8" ② ③ TA DA!

Meanwhile, mix together ½ - ¾ c rice or flax seeds, ¼ c lavender flowers, and a few drops of essential oil (the lavender/chamomile/mint mix, or whatever you prefer). Pour this stuff into the eye pouch and sew up the remaining side. Lay back and place this pillow over your eyes whenever you're suffering from headaches, insomnia, anxiety, or hangover.

If your headache is accompanied by an uncomfortable smothery feeling, you may have a sinus infection. These are usually treated with antibiotics. Whether or not you decide to take that route, here are some ways to make yourself more comfortable:

• Whenever you can, spend some time under a warm, steamy shower. This loosens mucus and makes blowing your nose easier.

• To make DIY mentholated rub, sans menthol, make a salve with eucalyptus, peppermint, basil, fennel, and some camphor if you can get it. Rub some on your chest and throat before you go to bed to ease congestion as you sleep.

• You can also use those same herbs, in essential oil form, to make bath salts. Add a drop or two of each oil to a cup of sea salt or epsom salts. Stir the salts into a steamy bath. Store in an airtight container if you're not using them right away.

• The best way to fight any sort of infection is to avoid excess stress on body systems, and to try and strengthen your immune system as much as you can. Immunity tonics can include herbs like echinacea, goldenseal, nettles and parsley. The latter two of these are full of vitamins & minerals and make a great tea (or salad) in their own right. Just make sure you cook or crush the stingers out of your nettles!

Echinacea

And now...

Natural Pain Relief! Thank God!

Sometimes you just feel crappy. Your back hurts or your head hurts or your uterus hurts and deep breathing alone is not cutting it. For those special moments, the following herbs can help:

White Willow Bark contains *salicylic acid,* which in 1853 was dismantled by French chemists and synthesized into what we know as aspirin. But folks were using the bark for centuries before that, as a painkiller, fever reducer, and anti-inflam-matory. White willow is best taken as a tea or a tincture, and should not be taken long term, as it can irritate your stomach like aspirin.

*Note: As with aspirin, white willow bark should not be given to young children.

Wild Lettuce is also called opium lettuce - guess why! Wild lettuce is most often used as an analgesic, sleep aid and sedative. Take as a tea or tincture.

Meadowsweet, like willow, contains salicylic acid, and unlike willow, it actually tastes pleasant. Make a tea out of the flowers, or chew a small hunk of peeled root.

Other helpful herbs include red raspberry, slippery elm, and valerian. I'll talk more about these in other sections.

Depression and anxiety

And now we come to what will most likely be the most earnest page of this book. Dealing with mental health issues in a holistic way is, I think, incredibly effective and heartening. But for the record, let me state that I am not in any way against using pharmaceuticals to treat depression. I know a lot of people find them creepy, oppressive, and over-prescribed. While I think that some of these criticisms are quite valid, I would also wager that few of the critics themselves have had to live with debilitating depression. My point is this: get help any way you can. If you try herbs and they don't work for your brain, get the help that is right for you. It doesn't make you weak and it doesn't mean you're selling out. Moving on...

St John's Wort is far and away the most popular herb for depression and/or anxiety. The SJW is most effective for mild to moderate depression, so it's perfect for people who want to manage depression but don't feel they need prescription meds. Try taking 15-30 drops of St John's Wort tincture in a cup of warm water, juice or tea 1-3 times each day.

St John's Wort

NOTE: This is important! If you take...

......birth control pills.....
......anti-depressants (prescription)......
......anti-coagulant meds (blood thinners).....
......certain HIV/AIDS meds......

...do not take St. John's Wort! Or use a condom! Compounds in SJW decrease the effectiveness of these medications. SJW can also make your skin more sensitive to sunlight, so wear sunscreen if you're taking it on a regular basis.

Other herbs that are good for depression include ginseng, licorice root, lemon balm and chamomile. Ginseng is good for foggy minds and lethargy, and is best used by folks whose depression does not include a lot of anxiety or restlessness. Licorice root is an allover glandular tonic and can help with hypothyroidic depression. Lemon balm and chamomile are both very calming, comforting herbs and are nice to take as a tea even if you're not depressed or anxious.

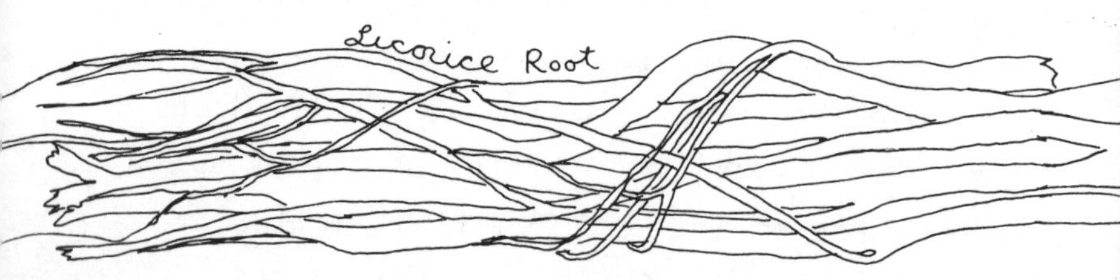

Before I end this section I wanted to mention two very effective and famous herbal sedatives: valerian root and kava root. Both of these are excellent soothers in times of stress or trauma.

Valerian is especially useful for insomnia*and menstrual cramps. The root is widely available and it's *seriously effective* - don't drive, bike, or operate a forklift after you take it. Valerian smells quite disgusting, so you will probably want to put your tincture in some juice.

FUN FACT Rats, cats and horses also respond to the effects of valerian.

Kava is a tropical root native to the Western Pacific. In a lot of cultures, kava holds a cultural importance not unlike that of alcohol or tea in other parts of the world; people drink kava beverages together in order to relax and enjoy each other's company. Kava is great because it relaxes you without sacrificing your mental clarity, so you can actually function. (It also numbs your mouth and throat a tiny bit, just to let you know.) Kava is available via mail order.

NOTE: There's been some controversy as to the effects of kava on the liver. If you are worried about this, practice moderation and do not combine kava with any sort of alcohol. Try a nice kava tea instead.

chapter 2
Nontoxic
Cleaning
+
Body
Care

Even if you really hate cleaning, I think most people will agree that having a clean and comfortable living space is lovely. Right? However, if TV and print ads are any indication, a lot of us have some seriously messed up ideas about dirt and cleanliness. We seem to think that in order to keep flesh-eating germs from devouring our families we need to bomb our houses and scrub our skins with antiseptic cleansers, the use of which mysteriously correlates with rising rates of chemical sensitivities and antibiotic-resistant supergerms. Plenty of folks are opting for the many "green" products popping up like weeds, but most of this stuff is too expensive to be accessible, or it's made by the same companies that make the mainstream products - so, even though you're trying not to, you're still giving them your money. It makes you wonder, are we really keeping ourselves healthy this way? Why on earth should we spend so much money just to make our lives comfortable?

Fortunately, there is a way to clean your home and your self without donning a fumigation suit: make your own cleaners! It's quite easy, and you'll be taking something practical and imbuing it with your own resourcefulness and creativity. That in itself is quite fulfilling.

Here are some more reasons to make your own cleaners:

• Sometimes germs are dangerous. But you know what's always dangerous? Neurotoxin! Chemicals like chlorine bleach, ammonia, and hydrochloric acid may be effective cleaning agents, but they are harmful to the nervous and respiratory systems, especially over long periods of exposure.

• For the price of a couple bottles of commercial product, you can keep yourself in DIY cleaners and body care for months + months. Plus, every ingredient in this chapter has tons of other uses.

• Homemade products are much gentler to folks who have sensitive skin or chemical sensitivities. They're also safer for kids and animals.

• The recipes in this book employ essential oils, herbs, and herbal infusions for their scents and chemical properties. So if you want your kitchen to smell like a lemon, or a forest, or a lemon forest, *it actually will!*

• Ingredients like castile soap and vinegar are gentle on the earth. Many soaps and detergents and cosmetics are made with byproducts of the oil industry, tested on animals, and then sold in a ridiculous amount of packaging. If you DIY, you can bypass this grossness and make biodegradable, ethical, and responsible products that you'll be proud to use!

basic ingredients for cleanin'

The following is a list of basic tools and ingredients that you'll need to make the recipes in this chapter. All of them should be available in any, well-stocked grocery store.

- vinegar (use cheap, white distilled vinegar unless specified) - cleanser, deodorizer, grease-cutter
- baking soda - deodorizer, mild abrasive
- ★ borax (aka $Na_2B_4O_7 \cdot 10H_2O$) - natural mineral disinfectant and cleanser
- salt - disinfectant, astringent, abrasive
- lemon juice - grease-cutter, cleanser, deodorizer
- ★ washing soda (aka sodium carbonate) - strips grease and wax, deodorizes
- castile soap - see my love letter on the next page
- essential oils - serve myriad purposes
- dried herbs
- cornstarch - absorbs oil, thickener
- hydrogen peroxide - disinfectant + non-chlorine bleach
- Vitamin C + aspirin - mild acids + exfoliants
- Canola oil - wood conditioner

★ = wear gloves when handling

In addition to these basic ingredients, you'll need some hardware. It's a good idea to take a thrifting trip and get these things even if you already have them, so you'll have some tools exclusively for DIY non-food purposes. If this is out of your budget, clean everything *very* well. Here's what you need:

- Ø measuring cups and spoons
- Ø at least one funnel
- Ø a mixing utensil (use non-reactive metal or plastic)
- Ø cheesecloth, muslin, or some old nylons - for straining stuff

- Ø a saucepan w/ a lid - enamel, glass or steel
- Ø an old blender or egg beater
- Ø latex gloves (to use when blending ingredients, if you have sensitive skin or are pregnant)

- Ø a buttload of containers, like:
  - spray bottles
  - squirt bottles
  - jugs
  - plastic tubs
  - squeeze bottles
  - dark glass bottles
  - pickle jars
  - mason jars

  ...and so on.

Castile

The name "castile soap" originally referred to a type of Spanish soap made from the area's native olive oil. Nowadays the name is given to any soap that is made with vegetable fats (usually hemp, palm, or olive oils) rather than animal fats like tallow. The result is soap in its gentlest, most basic form, which makes it ideal for cleaning pretty much everything. Not only is castile soap extremely versatile, it's cruelty-free, inexpensive, widely available, and in liquid form it's a great base for other herbal ingredients. You can usually find it under a couple different brand names at supermarkets, and in bulk at co-ops + health food stores.

I'm not going to provide a recipe for soap in this book - at least, not from-scratch soap. This chapter is about nontoxic cleaning, and all soaps are made with lye, a caustic alkaline that's about as toxic as you can get. I just didn't feel that it was a fitting recipe for this book. However, making your own soap <u>is</u> super fun and I urge you to take a class or check out a book on the subject, and learn to do it safely.

Soap!

Almost All-Purpose Spray Cleaner

1 t liquid castile soap
1 t borax
2 T white vinegar
2 c hot water
¼ t each eucalyptus and lavender oil
3 drops tea tree oil

• Mix all ingredients together in a spray bottle. You can use this on anything besides glass – spray it on, scrub, and rinse off with a clean, damp cloth.

Disinfecting Soft Soap

5 c grated soap (castile)
½ c baking soda
6 c hot peppermint or lemon peel tea
1 t eucalyptus essential oil
1 t borax

• Combine the soap and tea in a 3 quart stainless steel saucepan. Simmer 15 minutes on low heat, stirring occasionally. Add the remaining ingredients, one at a time. Stir well and, using a funnel, pour into a jug or squirt bottle. Shake well before using and apply with a sponge or brush.

Basic Window Cleaner

- 3 t liquid soap
- 3/4 c white vinegar
- 1/2 t baking soda
- 4-8 drops lemon oil

Combine all ingredients in a spray bottle. Shake well before using.

Mirror Cleaner

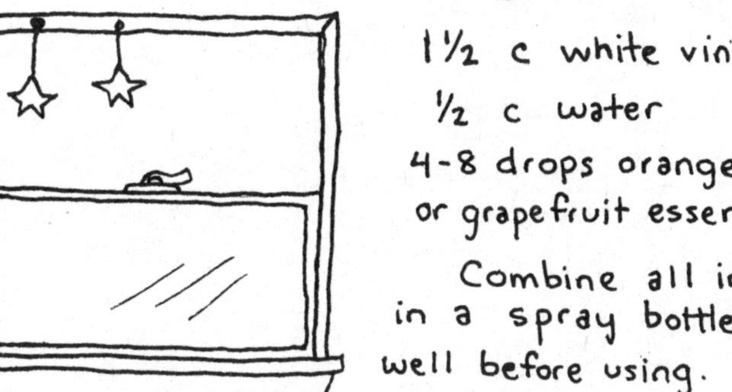

- 1 1/2 c white vinegar
- 1/2 c water
- 4-8 drops orange, lemon, or grapefruit essential oil

Combine all ingredients in a spray bottle. Shake well before using.

For both of these cleaners, just spray on + wipe off. But don't use paper towels! They're wasteful and they suck. Wipe off the cleaner with a soft, lint-free cloth or crumpled newspapers instead.

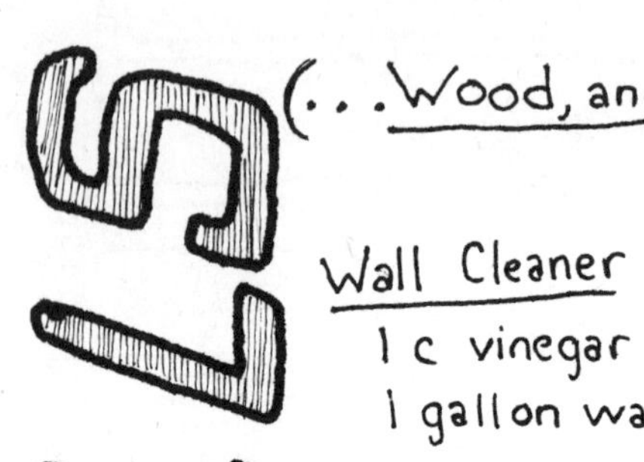

WALLS (. . . Wood, and Upholstery)

Wall Cleaner

1 c vinegar
1 gallon water

• Combine in a bucket & apply with a sponge.

*use this to shine + remove dust. For grimy walls, use Lemon Floor Cleaner on page 53

Gentle Wood Cleanser

½ c canola oil
¼ c liquid castile soap
¼ c water

• Combine and shake well before using. Apply with a rag, finish with a dry rag, and follow with polish.

Fabric Cleaner

1 c water
⅛ c liquid castile soap
½ t baking soda
1 T vinegar

• Combine in a spray bottle. Spray onto fabric, scrub with a sponge, and rinse with a little clean water. Blot with a clean rag.

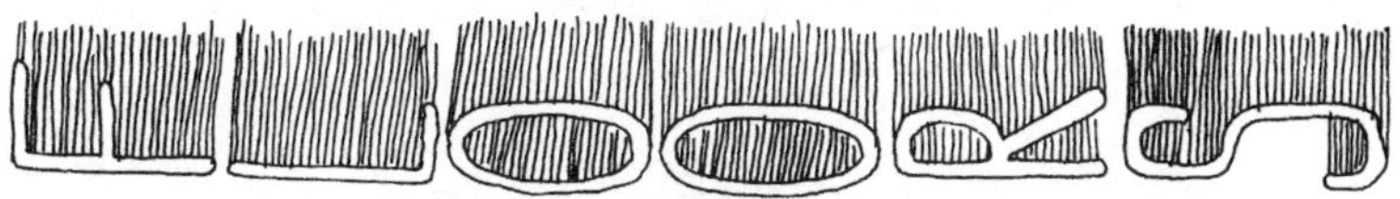

...of all varieties...

• WOOD FLOOR CLEANER •

1½ c water 1½ c vinegar 20 drops peppermint oil

– Combine all ingredients in a spray bottle. Use sparingly, spraying and dry-mopping as you go. Work on small sections of floor at a time. Give it another swipe with a dry mop to make the wood nice and shiny.

• LEMON FLOOR CLEANER •

1 c liquid castile soap
¼ c lemon juice
10 drops tea tree essential oil
6 c warm water

– Mix all ingredients and store in a plastic jug.

• PINE FLOOR CLEANER •

1 c liquid castile
½ c pine oil
6 c warm water

– Mix all ingredients and store in a plastic jug.

for vinyl and tile

• CARPET CLEANER •

3 c water ¾ c liquid castile 2-3 drops peppermint oil

– Mix all ingredients in a blender, until it is very foamy. Rub the foam into your carpet with a damp sponge, let dry and then vacuum.

• DRY METHOD FOR CARPET •

– Sprinkle the carpet with equal parts baking soda and borax, and then vacuum.

Liquid Dish Soap – not for the dishwasher!

Add up to 30 drops essential oil of your choice to 20 ounces liquid castile soap. I recommend citrus oils or lemon verbena for any sort of kitchen cleaner. If you use a soap that's already scented (like Dr. Bronner's), you can combine scents.

Sink Volcano! Sink Cleanser

¼ c baking soda   ½ c vinegar

Apply to a wet sink, scrub and rinse well.

DIY Drain Opener

Pour 1 c each salt + baking soda, plus ½ c vinegar down the drain. Let it sit for 15 minutes, and then flush the drain with 2-3 quarts of boiling water.

☆★ Add ½ c vinegar or lemon juice to your dishwater to help cut grease.★

toilets & tubs

Soft Scrub

1 c baking soda
¼ c liquid castile
3-5 drops tea tree oil
2 aspirins, powdered

Mix all ingredients together + add enough water to make a paste. Keep in a shampoo bottle. To use, apply with a sponge, scrub + rinse thoroughly.

Toilet Cleaner

2 c water
¼ c liquid castile
1 T tea tree oil or grapefruit essential oil

Combine everything in a spray bottle. Spray on ⇒ wipe off!

Bowl Cleaner - with SCIENCE!

½ c baking soda

¼ c vinegar

10 drops tea tree oil

Combine everything, pour into the toilet + scrub away.
Note: since this stuff explodes a little, each recipe = 1 cleaning.

★ To deodorize ★ curiously gross-smelling drains, sprinkle a handful of baking soda down the drain when it's dry ★

Laundry

All-Purpose Laundry Soap

This is a low-lathering, unscented detergent you can use in a washing machine. If you want to scent it, you can dry and pulverize some scented castile soap (like Dr. Bronner's) to use in the recipe, or add a few drops of your favorite essential oil.

This recipe makes enough for three loads, but is very easily doubled or tripled.

½ cup baking soda

½ cup powdered castile soap

¼ cup washing soda

¼ cup borax

*NOTE: In order for the soap powder to dissolve, use warm or hot water in your machine.

Mix ingredients well, add essential oils if you're using them, and stir again to break up any clumps.

Use ½ cup per load.

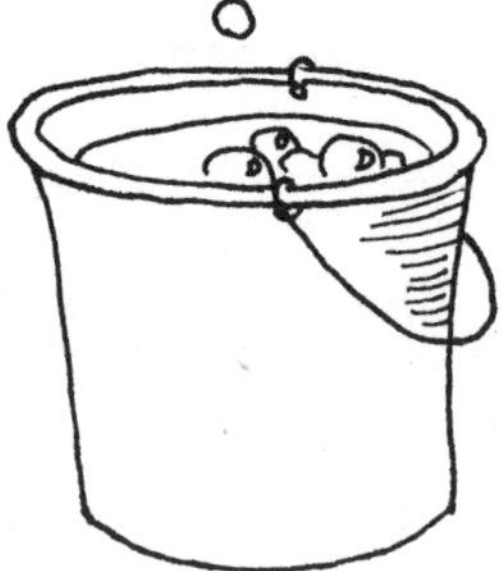

Fabric Softener Pouch

Technically this is a sachet—but I don't like the word "sachet." I like the word "**pouch**." First, make a pouch out of tightly woven fabric by folding a rectangle of cloth in half and sewing up the sides: ① ② BAM!

Make a couple of these and fill each with a couple spoonfuls of this mixture:

½ c baking soda

1 T arrowroot powder

1 T rice flour or cornstarch

1-3 drops essential oil (your choice)

Tie up the pouch tightly and pop it in the dryer with your clothes. Make a couple with different scents - lavender is nice for bedsheets and lemon verbena for clothing. Refill the pouch when the scent fades.

*A *sportive alternative:* let a couple of (clean) tennis balls bounce around with your laundry, to create air pockets and hence, fluffy freshness.

Homemade Bleach

1 c hydrogen peroxide
3 T lemon juice
15 c water

Mix all ingredients together + keep in a large plastic bottle.

Spray Starch

3 T plus 1 t cornstarch
4 cups warm water

Mix really well so no lumps remain, and keep in a spray bottle.

If you have a piece of clothing that bleeds or dyes your skin, try handwashing it with a few glugs of vinegar in the washwater.

Dry cleaning is kind of a scam. For most clothes that "require" dry cleaning, gentle hand-washing will suffice. Use All Purpose Laundry Soap or baby shampoo and dry it flat on a clean towel. Wool fibers like acid, so if you're washing wool, use castile and add vinegar to the soapy water.

Stain Removers

★ rub on your chosen antidote + launder as usual

★ Washing Soda is one of the best stain removers around. Make a paste with a little water and use it on:

- wine
- berries
- grease stains
- blood and other proteins
- coffee
- tea
- most other food stains
- sweat
- urine

★ Borax, like washing soda, is alkaline and thus dissolves acidic and protein-based stains, like the ones above. It also works really well on mildew. If you have hard water, use borax instead of washing soda, which will leave a chalky residue on fabric.

★ Vegetable oil is good for removing gummy labels and stickers.

★ Vinegar is acidic and removes alkalines like:

- grass
- rust
- paint
- ink

★ If you can't treat a stain right away, at least give it a rinse. Use only cold water, especially with proteins like blood. Heat will only cook the proteins and set the stain. Ew.

★ Glycerin is very sticky and slippery and is best used on oily or waxy stains, like lipstick.

★ Club soda will remove most of the stains listed under "washing soda." You can spray it on, dampen a towel with it, or just pour it on. It's a real amiable little product.

★ Once and for all: gum needs to be frozen and then pulled or chipped off. Smearing more crap on it does not work. Ok!

pest control

The key to keeping mice + bugs out of your space is to understand how they get in and why they want to be there. Once you know that, a bit of prevention and - sorry - scrupulous cleaning will keep them from hanging around.

- Your house is full of free food, so cover up your leftovers (and your kitchen's compost bin), wipe your counters, and take your trash + recycling out often. Don't leave food lying around, especially at night. The cleaner your place is, the less likely bugs are to inhabit it.

- Consider calling a truce with non-poisonous house spiders. They eat lots of flying insects, and contrary to popular belief, they hardly ever bite people.

- Keep potted plants or bundles of dried herbs around your kitchen, or wherever you're having an infestation. I keep most of my herbs in my kitchen and they've done a rad job of protecting my food against fruit flies. Bugs and mice especially hate: peppermint, oregano, basil, garlic, rosemary, lavender, lemon balm, hot peppers, and citrus peels.

- For nasty fruit fly infestations, make a trap: pour ½ inch of old wine in a jar, cover the mouth of the jar with plastic, and poke a few holes in the top. The flies'll be able to get in, and get drunk, but they won't come out.

Pest Repellant Powder

For flies, ticks, fleas, mosquitoes, roaches, ants, and mice – this just repels pests, it doesn't kill them.

2 handfuls dried peppermint
A healthy pinch each: garlic powder, cayenne, lavender flowers, lemon peel, and dried basil

Grind everything very finely and store in an airtight container. You can mix the herbs with some salt, if you like. Sprinkle the powder any place bugs like to hang out: in back of your cupboards, under your fridge/oven, around windows + doors, along baseboards, etc.

BIG GUNS! (If you need them)

- Borax is effective for killing bugs. Mix some with sugar and sprinkle it across doorways and along baseboards. Do <u>not</u> use this if you have kids or pets.

- You can spray lines of ants with diluted peppermint castile soap. The soap will kill the ants and erase the pheromone trail so other ants won't be able to follow.

- Make fly traps by painting strips of heavy paper with corn syrup or honey. Let it dry until it's tacky and then hang them up.

Random Messes
and how to destroy them

Lemon Rub for Copper + Brass

· Dip half a fresh lemon in salt and rub it over tarnished metal. Wash with soapy water, rinse and buff dry.

Oven Cleaner

· Scrub a *cold* oven with equal parts vinegar + water. If something spills in your oven, pour salt on the spill while the oven is still warm, and sweep out the salt with a brush when everything's cool.

Killing the Fridge Demon

· Clean your refrigerator's walls, shelves and drawers with a solution of ½ c water, 3 T baking soda, and 6 drops essential oil of your choice.

· To absorb weird smells, leave a small, open box of baking soda in a corner Of the fridge. Alternately, you can use a small bowl of coffee grounds (unused coffee grounds, thanks). These two tricks work well for musty freezers, also.

Gross Food Tips

- If your cooking pot is crusty with burnt stuff, scrub it with baking soda while it's still hot. Method 2: Use the pot to boil some water with a couple spoonfuls of baking soda thrown in. Let it sit until the food can be scraped off.
- For really greasy dishes, add ½ c lemon juice or vinegar to your dishwater.

Appliance Cleaner

- Mix together 2 parts each vinegar + lemon juice and 1 part water. Let sit on stains and scrub with a sponge. Don't leave your appliances plugged in when you clean them!

Cleaning a Coffeemaker

- Fill the coffee maker's water resevoir ¼ full with white vinegar, and add water until totally full. Turn the little guy on and let the cleaner drip into the pot. Turn the maker off and let it cool. Pour the vinegar-water solution back into the resevoir and let it cycle through again. Repeat once more. Pour out the vinegar solution and replace with clean water. Let that cycle through twice, and then wash both the coffee pot and the grounds basket in warm, soapy water.

oh, thank you!

Choosing Herbs for Your Skin & Hair

Here's a convenient table for when you're choosing oils or herbs to add to your formulations. Notice that rose, lavender, and licorice are excellent choices in any situation.

Herb/Oil	Oily	Dry	Sensi-tive	Anti-bacterial
Aloe Vera		★		
Birch				★
Calendula		★	★	
Chamomile		★	★	
Cinnamon				★
Comfrey		★	★	
Eucalyptus				★
Horsetail	★	★		
Lavender	★	★	★	★
Lemon Balm	★			
Lemon Verbena	★			
Lemongrass				★
Licorice	★	★	★	
Mint	★	★		
Nettle		★		
Orange Blossom		★		
Rose	★	★	★	★
Rosemary	★			★
Sage	★			
St. John's Wort		★		
Sweet Orange				★
Tea Tree	★			★
Thyme				★
Witch Hazel	★			

basic shampoo + body soap

Remember that bottle of castile soap you used to clean your whole living space? Pour some on your head! Castile soap is so basic that it can clean pretty much any part of you besides your eyeballs. To make a gentle soap for your hair and skin, mix 12 oz. of unscented castile soap with up to 30 drops of an essential oil or oils suitable for your hair and skin type. Cap the bottle, give it a shake, and that's it!

... Except, not really. You see, regular shampoos do not contain soap, they contain detergents like the dreaded ☠ sodium laureth sulfate ☠, or SLS. For a while people thought SLS caused cancer. For the most part that idea has been debunked, but it is still true that SLS is rather irritating to skin.

Detergents like SLS are cheap, very foamy, and very effective, because they strip oil and dirt from surfaces (your dishes, your clothes, or your face) and then rinse clean. Castile soap, on the other hand, does not strip oils quite as well, and is much gentler on your skin. The downside to all this loving gentleness is that castile can leave a bit of residue on your hair.

A lot of folks don't mind this, or even prefer it, but if you want that squeaky-clean feeling, you'll have to cut the residue with a mild acid. Try rinsing your hair with a coffeemug-full of diluted lemon juice or vinegar after you shampoo. Make sure to rinse again with clean water if you don't want to smell like a gherkin.

Soapwort Shampoo

Soapwort is a funny little shrub that contains natural saponins (soap-like chemicals) which cause the flesh of the plant to lather when agitated.

A decoction of soapwort root (or its tropical neighbor, soap bark) can be used as a gentle cleanser for hair and skin. The nettles in this recipe add shine + body to hair, and the lemon verbena smells nice.

* NOTE: this will not be as foamy as regular shampoo, so don't worry if you can't work up a huge lather with this stuff.

2 c distilled water
1½ T dried, chopped soapwort root
1 t dried (2 t fresh) lemon verbena
1 t dried nettles
Optional: a couple drops of essential oil suitable for your hair type

1. Get yourself a big jar with a lid, put the soapwort root and water inside, and let it soak overnight.

2. In the morning, pour the whole mess into a saucepan and bring it to a boil. Reduce the heat to low, cover, and let simmer for 20 minutes.

3. Remove the pan from the heat and add nettles and lemon verbena. Mix well and allow to cool completely.

4. Line a funnel with cheesecloth (several layers), muslin, or the foot from an old pair of nylons. Place the spout of the funnel in a squirt or pump bottle and decant your new shampoo. Squeeze the solids to get out the last bit of liquid before tossing.

5. If you're using essential oils, add them now. Cap the bottle and give it a good shake.

★ This shampoo keeps for up to 10 days on the shelf, a day or two longer in the fridge. You can take advantage of this and make a really nice shampoo to use in the summer. Replace the nettles in the recipe with some nice invigorating rosemary, and add a couple drops of tea tree or peppermint essential oil at the end. Keep it in the fridge and use it any time you need a cheap (and homemade!) thrill.

Baking Soda Shampoo

I don't think this even counts as a recipe. Basically: try using baking soda instead of shampoo. Just rub a couple teaspoons of baking soda into the roots of your hair while it's wet, and rinse off in the shower. The soda will clean your hair and dissolve any product build-up. If you really like using liquid shampoo, you might also try mixing a teaspoon each of baking soda and shampoo and using that to wash your hair. The combination of the two is awesome for dissolving serious product build-up.

Homemade Conditioners

→ aka *Godsend or Greasehead?*

I have tried many homemade conditioners in my time, including olive oil, egg yolks, mayo, mashed bananas, and avocado. And I always end up with stubborn chunks of fruit, cooked eggs, or ungodly amounts of grease in my hair. I'm not saying that egg yolks don't work, just that I personally always screw them up; because of this, I don't really feel comfortable suggesting that you put that stuff on your head. What I am going to suggest is that you may not need a conditioner... *at all*! Scandal!

But think about it: commercial shampoos are designed to strip the scalp of the oil it naturally produces, and conditioners are supposed to replace those oils with fruity, pearly goodness. But if you switch your shampoo with a head soap that doesn't strip those oils, why would you need all that extra moisturizer on your head? Makes sense, right? Of course, if you have coarse, thick or dry hair, or you wash your hair often, you'll probably want a conditioner at least some of the time. And here comes one right now!

Vinegar Rinse + Conditioner

4 c very hot water
3/4 c vinegar (cider is nice)
2 T each dried nettles, dried rosemary, and dried chamomile flowers

- Tie the herbs up in a bit of muslin and combine with the other ingredients in a jar. Cover + let steep overnight. In the morning, remove the herb bag. To use, work in up to a cup of the vinegar after you shampoo, and rinse well.

Facial Cleansers

Homemade face soaps are wonderful not only because making and using them is so satisfying, but because they cost a fraction of the price of drugstore cleansers. You can make a big batch of simple cleanser and add different ingredients according to your changing skin, the seasons, your mood, anything!

Simple Face Soap

1 oz grated bar soap - homemade, castile, or your favorite purchased soap, or liquid soap

2 c hot herbal infusion, made with herbs suitable for your skin type, or plain water

Combine soap + water in a jar + let sit overnight so the soap can dissolve. To use, massage a bit into your skin and rinse with water. If you want a foamier cleanser, increase the amount of soap. Other ways to customize:

- add up to five drops of suitable essential oil.
- add witch hazel extract for oily skin, glycerin or honey for dry skin
- add baking soda to make a paste-y, scrubby cleanser
- crush two aspirins into powder and add to the soap to make a cleanser for pimply skin.
- increase the amount of soap in the recipe and use antiseptic herbs and oils to make an antibacterial wash for hands and minor injuries.

Creamy Lavender Cleanser

1 part each: jojoba oil
glycerin (found at drugstores)
cornstarch

3 drops lavender oil

Combine ingredients in a bowl and mix until smooth + creamy. Transfer to a small jar. To use, rub some into your skin, wipe it off with a soft cloth, and rinse well. This cream is like a nice, light cold cream. Since it contains no beeswax or lanolin, it's easy to rinse off and is naturally vegan–just make sure your glycerin is vegetable-derived.

* Rose & Honey Face Wash *

½ c rose water; homemade is best
2 T liquid castile soap
1 t honey
up to 5 drops rose essential oil (optional)

This is easiest if the rose infusion is still warm. Combine the rose water and honey and stir until the honey is dissolved. Add the soap and oils and mix well. Store in a pump bottle and use by rubbing the liquid over your skin and rinse with warm water. This recipe can also be added to your bathwater.

herbal toners ...in your face!

Herbal infusions are really terrific for treating conditions like acne, rosacea, dryness, and so on. If your skin is troubling you, splash or rub some herb-infused water, vinegar, or diluted tincture on your skin after you wash it. Here are some suggested combinations:

• ACNE: peppermint + birch bark-infused vinegars with a few drops of lavender oil

• ALSO ACNE: witch hazel extract infused with sage and lemon balm, plus 10 drops tea tree oil (per cup of infusion)

• ECZEMA: strong infusion of equal parts chamomile, nettles, and calendula, with about a spoonful of Epsom salts dissolved in it

• DRY SKIN: rose-infused water with a spoon-full of honey and a few finely-ground almonds

• IRRITATED SKIN: equal parts water and aloe vera juice. Infuse the water with comfrey and calendula.

• ROSACEA: water or vinegar infused with oatmeal (wrap some in a bag, like you're making tea), chamomile and licorice.

• ROUGH SKIN: vinegar infused with birch bark, rose, and chamomile flowers. You can also replace the birch bark with one or two crushed aspirin tablets.

Exfoliation and Other Pleasures

There are basically two ways to exfoliate your skin. *Mechanical scrubs* rely on small particles, like sand, salt, and ground-up plant parts, to create friction that rubs off dead skin cells. Loofahs and brushes work in the same way. Abrasives also increase blood flow to the skin. Even if you don't care about stuff like exfoliation, I heartily recommend giving yourself a good scrub now and then. I use a stiff-bristled brush on my skin every morning before I shower and it makes a huge difference in how awake I feel.

Chemical scrubs, even hundred-dollar schmancy ones, generally depend on hydroxy acids, which work by dissolving the intercellular glue between bits of dead skin. Hydroxy acids are present in many fruits, milk, sugar and other plants like birch. They're seriously everywhere; it's pretty ridiculous that people pay so much money to get them in a jar.

Some notes:

- If you have sensitive skin, avoid really grainy scrubs.
- Scrubs + brushes/loofahs work best on dry skin.
- If you're scrubbing your whole body, do your legs first, then your arms, then your torso. Always rub towards your heart, and be gentle with the skin atop your vital organs.

Scrubby Scrubs

The instructions for all of these are the same: just rub the scrub around on your skin for about 20 seconds (or whatever), and rinse well. Most can be used for face and body; the exceptions would be very coarse, salt-based scrubs, which you should keep to below the neck.

★ for oily skin ★

- baking soda, a crushed aspirin, and enough water to make a paste
- handful of seasalt + 1 T ground sage, moistened with birch or lavender infusion
- sugar moistened with lemon juice
- still-damp coffee grounds (used)
- equal parts milk powder and honey, plus a little lemon juice and cornmeal
- sea salt with 2 drops teatree oil

★ for normal skin ★

- equal parts ground oatmeal and plain yogurt
- a handful of cornmeal moistened with honey
- a slushee of sugar and almond oil or aloe vera gel
- ground dried adzuki beans and a pinch of dried calendula petals, + a little water
- rice flour, a tiny bit of liquid soap, and water
- one or two ground aspirins and a dab of honey
- brown sugar a pinch of ground rose petals, and a wee bit of apple cider vinegar
- sea salt, zest from one lemon, and almond oil

★ for dry skin ★

- equal parts honey and finely-ground almonds
- sea salt + a few drops essential oil + enough olive oil to make a thick slush
- 1/2 an avocado with enough oat flour to make a paste
- ground flax seeds and a little rose water
- 2 T each ground oats and almonds + 1 T rose water + 1 T heavy cream
- equal parts plain yogurt and ground almonds
- a little plain yogurt mixed with the contents of 1 bag of green tea (about 1 tablespoon).

super precious face oil

This is the stuff I use on my face every day. I love using it: the bergamot, lavender, and clary sage oils make me feel happy and relaxed, and using a dropper makes me feel like a scientist. If you keep this oil in dark glass and away from heat and light, it will last you a very long time.

2 oz carrier oil (see below)
15 drops essential oil(s) suitable for your skin

For oily skin, use grapeseed oil, hazelnut, or jojoba oils

For normal skin, use almond, jojoba, or apricot kernel oil

For dry skin, use olive, coconut, or macademia nut oil. For really dry skin, mix in some avocado oil also.

Combine the ingredients in a small bowl and funnel it all into a dark glass bottle with a dropper. To use, combine 2-3 drops of oil with 4 drops of warm water. Rub your hands together to emulsify the oil, and pat it on your face until it's absorbed. You can change the ratio of oil to water depending on how dry your skin is.

Some suggestions for essential oils:

- Oily skin: 5 drops each rosemary, clary sage, and bergamot oils
- Normal skin: 5 drops each rose, lavender, and peppermint oil
- Dry skin: 5 drops each chamomile, rose, and orange blossom oil

Peppermint

Easy Deodorant Powder

• Combine equal parts cornstarch and baking soda and add a few drops of an antibacterial essential oil like lavender or tea tree. Store in an air-tight jar to preserve the scent. You can slap this on wherever you like – put it on with a powder puff, if you're fancy.

* reduce the amount of baking soda in this recipe to make body powder, which absorbs moisture + prevents chafing

DIY Toothpaste

2 oz chalk (calcium carbonate - found @ hardware stores and online)
1 oz baking soda
Pinch stevia powder (for sweetness)
Vegetable glycerin
5-6 drops peppermint oil

• Combine dry ingredients and oils with enough glycerin to make a paste. Keep the paste in an airtight jar, along with a little spoon to get the paste onto your brush.

• Other good oils include cinnamon, rose, clove, and lemon

• Yes, just plain baking soda (or soda + stevia + peppermint oil) is an easy and effective alternative to this recipe.

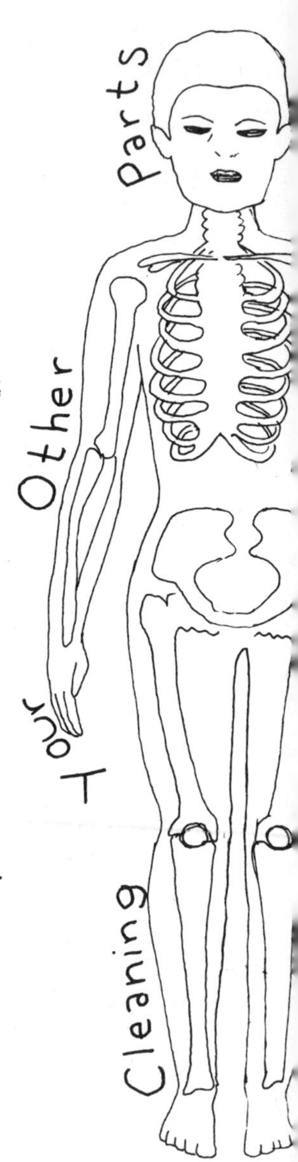

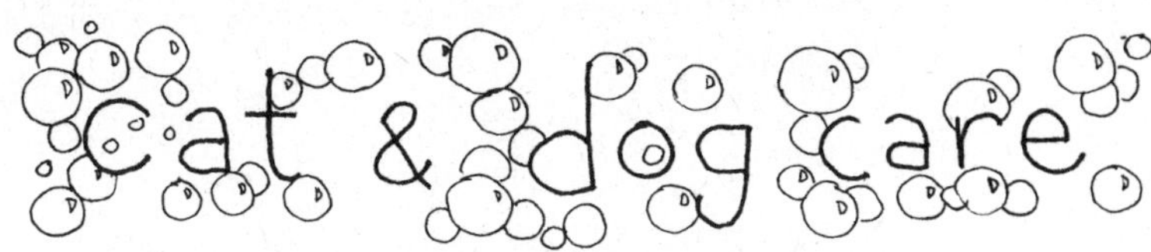

Basic Dog (and cat) Shampoo

1½ T castile soap - use lightly scented or unscented soap
1½ c warm water

Combine soap + water in a jar + shake to combine. Dampen your dog's fur, rub in the shampoo, and rinse thoroughly. Make sure not to get this in your dog's eyes - use a soapy washcloth to clean his/her face.

If this soap leaves a residue on your dog's fur, rinse with a cup of vinegar diluted in water.

Fancy: replace the warm water with an infusion of half lavender and half rose geranium. This will help repel fleas and ticks.

Dry Shampoo for Cats...and people!

½ c cornstarch
2 T lavender flowers, ground fine

Sprinkle some of this on your cat's fur, rub it in, and brush out after an hour or so.

★ **NOTE**: Avoid using essential oils on animals. If you really feel you need to use them, make sure they're heavily diluted - no more than 1 drop oil to 1 cup of carrier.

chapter 3

Gardening

Other than killing stuff, making tools, and breeding more of ourselves, gardening is our most enduring hobby as a species. No wonder, then that it can get so incredibly complicated! In researching this chapter, I encountered more techniques, tips, and fussy projects than I thought possible for a process that Nature seems so capable of handling by herself. Human ingenuity, man. And while I think all that stuff is incredible, this chapter will be a very simple affair about growing vegetables. Make that: growing vegetables cheaply and organically. Because what's more DIY than that? It's the greatest nesting skill on Earth! Or at least, it's something that's always interested me, and if you're reading this, it probably interests you too. Ok? Ok!

* Super shoutout: this chapter depended heavily on the superb expertise of my dear friend Ivy Fox, who is a phenomenal gardener and an even better friend. Thanks girl! *

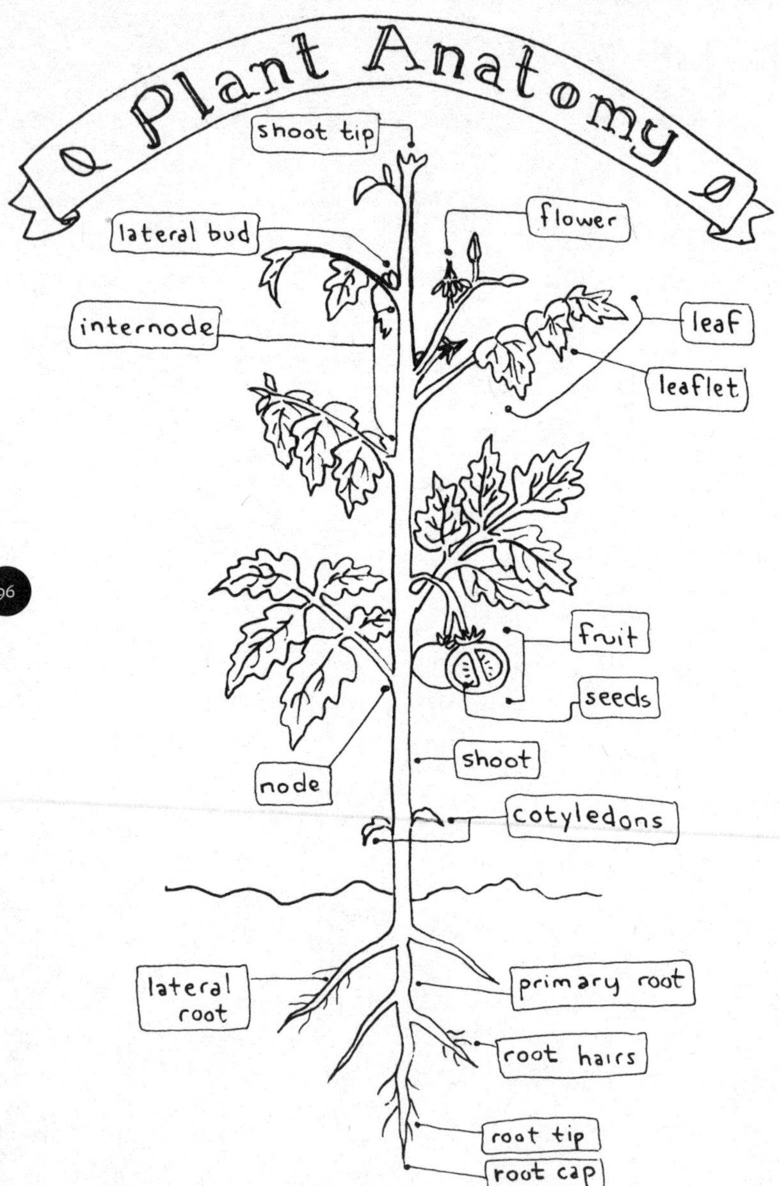
Plant Anatomy
shoot tip
flower
lateral bud
internode
leaf
leaflet
fruit
seeds
shoot
node
cotyledons
lateral root
primary root
root hairs
root tip
root cap

A (very) Brief Glossary* of Gardening Terms

- **Annual**: a plant that completes its life cycle within one year. The life cycle being:

seed → plant → flower → fruit → dead → seed

This means you'll have to plant these every year. It also means that if you don't like something, it's not going to stick around forever. Most vegetables are annuals, and are separated by season and hardiness (frost tolerance). Examples:

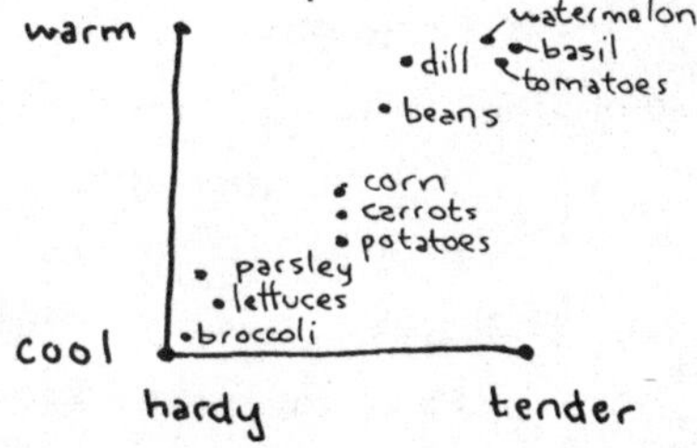

- **Perennial:** a plant that dies down to the ground in winter but keeps its roots alive underground, allowing it to grow back in the spring. There are only a few perennial vegetables (rhubarb, asparagus, artichokes) but many perennial herbs, including:

  - lavender, thyme, chives, oregano, sage, mint, lemon balm, rosemary, tarragon

Perennials can tolerate a lot more and are generally less wussy than annuals, so consider making a permanent place in your life for them. They also make excellent houseplants!

• **NPK**: if you're shopping for fertilizer you'll see this acronym alot. NPK stands for nitrogen (N), phosphate (P), and potash or potassium (K), which are the three main nutrients plants need. On the fertilizer package you'll also see a number like 10-10-10 or 5-10-5. This refers to the proportion of each nutrient in the fertilizer mix.

• **Mulch**: a material spread over soil in order to maintain the soil's integrity. Mulch helps keep in moisture, maintain a steady temperature, and it keeps weeds from germinating; basically, it's a blanket for your garden. If you want to mulch, make sure you do it when your garden soil is just how you like it – if you mulch overly damp, cold soil, it will stay that way. Some materials that make good mulch: straw, compost, grass clippings, shredded newspaper, gravel, wood chips, and pine needles.

• **Aeration**: the process of loosening soil by digging or tilling. Aerating your soil decompacts dirt and allows air to pass through soil particles.

• **Cultivar**: this term refers to a variety of plant originated by gardeners instead of in the wild.

• **Heirloom**: the definition of an heirloom is hotly debated, but generally, an heirloom is a very old (like, at least 50 years old) cultivar that is not a hybrid.

Assessing your Space

Regardless of whether you are planning to garden in your backyard, your windowsill, or a vacant lot, the first thing you need to do is to take a census of your space and its resources. Here's a list of questions to ask yourself when you're looking around:

Space

• How big is your proposed garden or container? Do you have enough room for a mature root structure? If you want to grow tall plants, do you have the required vertical space?

Sunlight

• When will your garden get direct sunlight? Are there any pesky shade trees or tall buildings nearby? How many sunny days do you get during the warm season?

Water

• Is there a hose or other water source nearby? Is your local climate rainy or arid? How much time are you willing to spend watering? Do you plan to use greywater in your garden?

Soil

• Do you know what kind of soil is prevalent in your area? What other plants are growing in your neighborhood? If you wet down your lawn, how quickly does it dry out again?

Weather & Climate | ... & Landscape

• Is your area prone to drought, tornadoes, heavy rains or other ill weather? If so, how protected is your garden? Do you live in a city? Do you have to worry about pipes/neighbors/car exhaust? Does your area have any invasive species that should be avoided (like English Ivy in the Northwest U.S.)?

Pests

• Do you know what creatures are waiting to eat your plants? Is your area rural enough to be home to larger herbivores, like rabbits or deer? And what about plant diseases? Are there any that your region is particularly vulnerable to?

I know this self-quiz seems really long, but don't fret - these questions are really just a way for you to remember all the little specifics which seem obvious in retrospect ("I planted roses in the desert and I'm sick of watering them!") but are easy to forget. Doing as much trouble-shooting as you can before you plant will save you a lot of grief later on. If that makes your brain hurt, here are good rules of thumb:

• grow your vegetables on level ground, or in rows cutting across the slope of the ground, to prevent soil erosion.

• make sure your plots are near a water source; use greywater only on non-edibles.

• Vegetables and other edibles will grow best if they get at least 8 hours of sunlight each day, so choose a spot that's not shaded over by trees, buildings, or other structures.

When to plant

Unfortunately, if you're growing stuff outside, you can't really just stick a few seeds in the ground in January and wait for a zucchini to pop out. Different plants have different seasons based on their ability to handle low temperatures, frost, and so on. If you know when to plant each veggie you'll be able to maximize the plant's yield and eat much better. I wish I could draw a little chart and just tell you when to plant what, but alas, I don't know where you live. So you'll need to do two things:

1. If you live in the US, figure out which USDA zone you live in. The USDA splits the nation into 11 "hardiness zones" based on average minimum temperatures. It's kind of an old system, since it was introduced before most people gave a crap about factors like pollution. But gardeners and farmers still use it. You can

find this map in almost any gardening book or website, and on the USDA's website (which also has lots of information about specific crops, invasive species, and, uh, corn prices).

The map is swirly and colorful and would make a really rad poster. Once you know your zone, you can look up a planting schedule, which will tell you stuff like:

- a plant's frost tolerance and the length of its season;
- minimum soil and air temperatures for many different vegetables; and
- the best times of year to start seeds (more on that later) and to plant them in the ground.

You can look up planting schedules online or in a farmer's almanac. If you live outside the US, check your government's agricultural agency for information on planting.

A lot of gardeners like to apply a more intuitive approach to timing, because it fosters a deeper connection between them and the earth. I think that's really lovely; but I also think that beginning food-growers should try planting by the books for a year or two and then work from there.

Making Beds

If you only do two things to your garden, let them be these: ① work some compost into your soil, and ② build a raised and/or sunken bed. Why? Because I like watching you sweat! Just kidding. Because adjusting the height of your garden can solve a lot of problems. A raised bed will increase drainage, reduce the number of weeds, snails and slugs amongst your veggies, and will make gardening more accessible to folks with limited mobility. A sunken bed will help sandy or otherwise dry soil retain moisture + nutrients. Whichever style you choose, you will need some rot-resistant wood (like red cedar) if you can get it. You can certainly use any untreated lumber you like, but tough woods like cedar will make for long-lasting beds. Depending on how high you want your bed to be, you can use one plank per side, or stack them. Length and width are also up to you, but keep in mind that if you can't reach the middle of the bed you're going to feel silly. 6' x 4' is a good bed size, and you can certainly make more than one per yard. If all types of wood are beyond your budget, cement blocks are an easy, scavenge-able alternative, as are bricks and stones joined with or without mortar.

① Plot the size and shape of your bed by pounding in some wooden stakes at the corners of the planned bed. String rope or twine between the stakes.

② Inside this shape, dig up as much vegetation as you can. If you're not planning to plant for a few months, you can cover the ground with plastic to kill off any weeds. Leave the plastic on for 2 months or so. Once you have a bare patch of earth, work it well with a shovel.

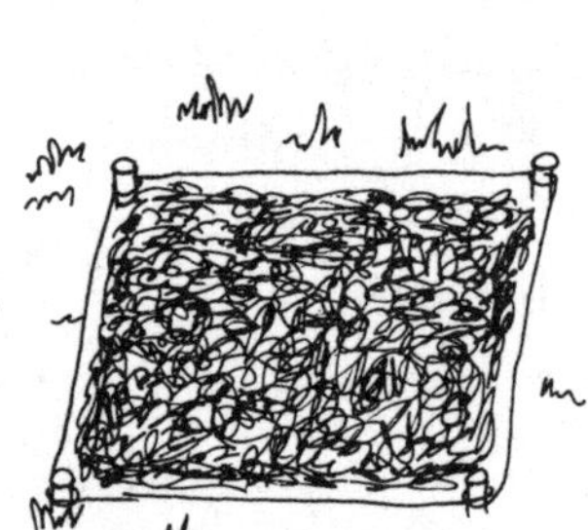

③ Place your planks with their long ends against the stakes. Get a friend to help you hold the planks while you check the tops of the planks with a level (if you care). Secure the planks to the stakes with wood screws. If you like, you can tack on some metal brackets outside

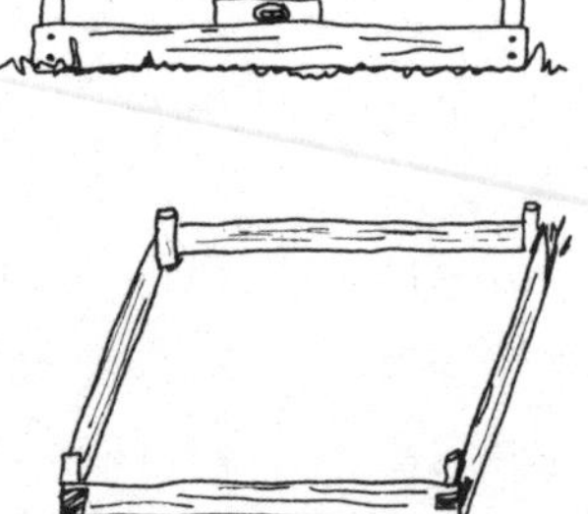

the frame using wood screws or nails.

④ If you're making a very tall bed, keep stacking + securing planks atop the first until the bed is as high as you'd like it to be.

⑤ Time to fill your bed! You can use soil from other parts of your yard, potting mix, layers of dirt and compost and mulch - whatever you like!

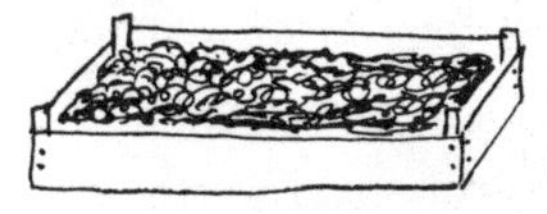

If you want to build a sunken bed, the process is similar. Basically, you'll need to dig out a very large, shallow hole, place the stake-and-plank frame inside it, and tamp the dirt down around the outside of the frame.

★ A pretty awesome amendment to a raised bed: a tiny greenhouse! Collect a couple of hula hoops of equal diameter, saw each in half, tape or otherwise secure their feet to a couple of 2×4"s (as shown), and cover the whole thing with plastic! RAD.

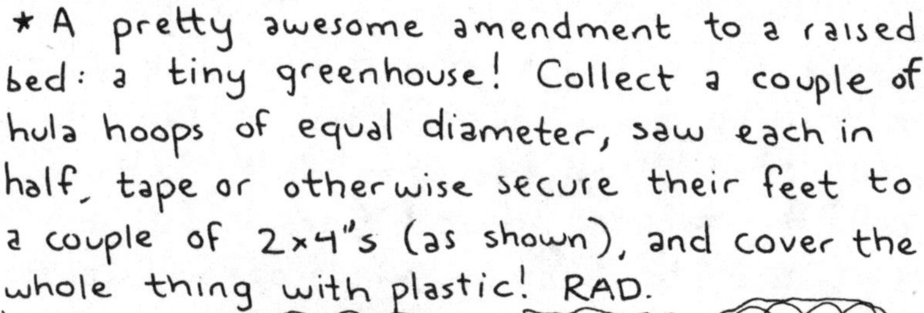

tips for garden layout

Make sure beds are at least a foot and a half apart from each other, so you have someplace to walk. Planks or flat rocks will keep it dry.

• Plant as far as you can away from trees and shrubs. Not only will they shade your garden, their roots will suck up water + nutrients.

• Keep annuals and perennials in separate beds or in separate areas of the garden. Woody herbs, for example, need less water than many annuals, and in the fall, you'll be able to clean up your annual beds without disturbing the still-living perennials.

• Plant your tallest veggies (corn, trellised vines, etc.) at the north end of your garden, and your low-growers at the south end. This way all your plants get that lovely southern sun.

• Save very sunny spots for fruit-bearing plants and roots. A good rule is that if a plant is made up mostly of green leaf, it can tolerate more shade than one that isn't. Lettuces, collards, cabbages and so on grow well in partial shade because the large surface area of their leaves makes for maximum sunlight absorbtion.

• Try your hand at companion planting: plant rows of early bloomers like salad greens and radishes in between rows of long-term crops like peppers. You'll save a ton of space this way, because you'll harvest those short-term veggies before the peppers are big enough to need that extra room.

• If your goal is to actually subsist mainly on your garden, plant several varieties of a vegetable you eat a lot, like an onion or carrot. The different plants will take varying lengths of time to mature, so you'll have a steady income of onions over a couple months instead of a buttload of them in the same week.

• Annual veggies are basically divided into cool season crops and warm season crops. You can start early in the year and plant a quick-growing crop, harvest in the spring and immediately replace it with a summer crop. Repeat in the fall with some hardy broccoli or root veggies, and you'll get three harvests out of one patch of dirt. CHA-CHING!

• Herbs are awesome to have in your garden, but certain types can get way out of control. Mint and yarrow are notorious for this. Consider keeping a separate bed for herbs, or even better, plant herbs in containers, inside or outside your home.

The Buddy System

Plants are sort of like superheroes: each has its own specialty (bug-repelling, nitrogen-fixing, etc.), but when you let them hang out together, those advantages are compounded. Try using plant buddies if you find yourself using a lot of fertilizer or bug spray.

Plant	Good Buddies	Bad Buddy
Beans	carrots, corn, radishes, peas, lettuce	onions
Beets	beans (bush), cabbage, onions	
Cabbage	beets, celery, onions, tomatoes	strawberry
Carrots	beans, lettuce, peas, radishes, tomatoes	
Corn	beans, squash, melons, peas	
Cucumber	beans, corn, lettuce, onions, radishes	strong herbs
Lettuce	carrots, cukes, radish, strawberries	
Melons	corn, radishes	
Onions	beets, carrots, celery, cucumber, peppers, tomatoes, squash	beans, peas
Peas	beans, carrots, radishes, turnips	onions
Peppers	onions	
Radishes	beans, carrots, melons, lettuce	
Spinach	celery, eggplant, cauliflower	
Squash	corn, onion, radishes	
Strong Herbs	cabbage, peppers, tomatoes	cucumber
Strawberry	beans, lettuce, onion, spinach	cabbage
Tomatoes	cabbage, carrots, spinach	corn
Zucchini	corn, onions, radishes	

dirt aint dirt: testing and improving your soil

There are several soil-based factors that influence which plants will grow where. The first of these is soil texture or composition. Besides bugs, rocks and roots, soil is generally made up of clay, silt, and sand. If you have very sandy or clayey soil, it's going to change what kind of care you give your plants and what will grow well there. Here are two ways to test your soil's texture:

Method 1: Dirt Ballin'

· Grab a handful of recently-watered soil and roll it into a little ball. If it holds tightly and is tacky to the touch, you have clay soil. If it will not stick together and is sharp or gritty-feeling, it's sandy soil. If it holds somewhat and feels soft, like a river bed, it's mostly silt.

Method 2: Dirt Parfait!

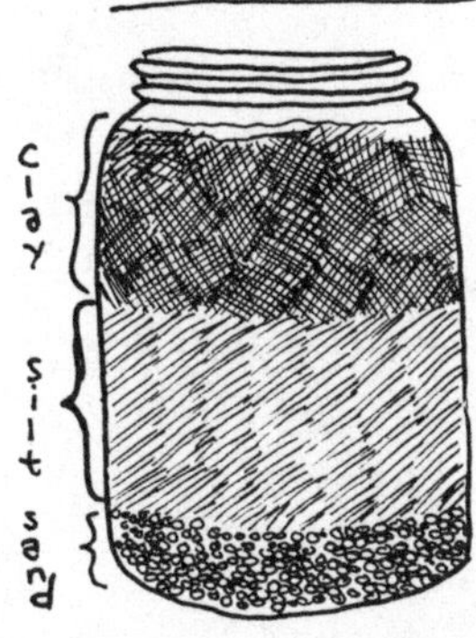

· Fill a large jar 2/3 full with water. Add a squirt of dish soap and fill the jar the rest of the way with dirt. Shake well and let settle for 2 days. The dirt will separate into three layers as shown at left. Naturally, the biggest layer is what your soil is mostly made of.

If what you see in your jar has about equal parts sand and silt, with slightly less clay, congratulations! This means you've got loam soil, which is very nice soil indeed: it drains well and also retains needed moisture and nutrients. Don't freak if you don't have loam soil! You can still have a rad garden – you just need to either adjust your soil or reconsider what plants you want to grow. To adjust very clayey or sandy soils, work compost into the first foot or so of soil. If your beds are still too moist, consider building raised beds to increase drainage. If your soil needs constant watering, a sunken bed can help.

An alternative to all of this is to simply sow plants that like to live in the type of soil you have. This might narrow your choices a bit, but it's a very sustainable way to garden. For sandy soil, try planting:

- root vegetables, vines and leafy veggies, like:
  - tomatoes
  - squashes
  - potatoes
  - carrots
  - spinach
  - peppers
  - strawberries
  - corn
  - lettuces

★keep in mind that sand drains quickly and if you don't build a sunken bed, you'll have to water often.

★nutrients leach quickly in sandy soil, so you might need to fertilize more often

For heavy clay and silt soils, plant these:

- shallow rooted plants, like pear trees
- virtually all members of the large + tasty Brassicaceae family:
  - broccoli
  - cauliflower
  - cabbages
  - kohlrabi
  - kale
  - Brussels sprouts

- clay soil is fertile and nutrient-rich, but does not drain well. If you don't build a raised bed, work your soil well to decompact it, and cut down on your watering.

Once you've worked out your soil texture, you need to determine its pH. On the standard pH scale, ideal soil is about here:

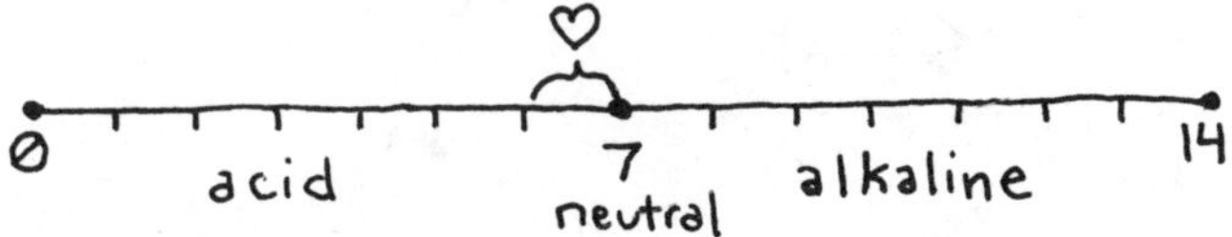

To test your pH, get a kit from a garden store, or send a jar of dirt to your local county extension office for testing (www.csrees.usda.gov/Extension).

- Very alkaline soil can be corrected by working in sawdust, wood chips, or partially rotted leaves.
- Very acidic soil can be corrected by adding crushed oyster shells or wood ashes.
- An inch of compost worked into the soil will balance slightly acidic or alkaline soil. It will also improve drainage, fertility, and everything else!

Compost for beginners

Everyone loves composting. It's a fact! Tending a compost heap is the easiest, cheapest, most environmentally sound way to create healthy soil for your garden. If you don't already have a compost pile in your yard or apartment complex, here's how it should go down:

① Grab a trash bag and a bucket. Use the bag(s) to collect stuff like paper scraps, straw, dead leaves, and other dry material. What you'll have is a bag full of carbon-rich substance that will form the base of your compost.

Meanwhile, fill the bucket with nitrogen-rich matter like grass clippings, food scraps, aged manure (see note), and so on. Many of my friends keep a lil' bucket under their sink just for compost fodder. FYI, you can also compost:

- bread products
- egg- and nutshells
- flat beer
- lint
- wood ashes
- junk mail (shredded)

② Find a spot in your yard and, if you wish, build an enclosure for your compost. You could buy one, of course, but it's just as easy to nail some pallets together, or bend some wire mesh into a cylinder. A big pile in a corner of the yard is also fine.

③ To build your compost, start with a bed of dry, carbon-y stuff about 6 inches deep. On top of that, spread a 2 inch deep layer of nitrogen material. Then, the icing, as it were: a shovelfull of dirt from your garden. The garden soil will introduce the organisms that will be making your compost.

④ Repeat these three layers until the pile is about three feet tall. This part goes by very quickly if you have some friends and a couple of extra shovels. Try to keep the ratio of dry stuff to moist stuff at around 3:1.

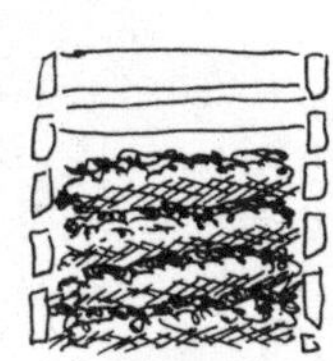

⑤ Water your compost until the whole thing is just damp, but not wet.

⑥ Over the next couple of months, this pile should get quite warm. This is a good sign, as it signals that decomposition is taking place. If, after a month, it's not warm at all, add some more moist, rotting vegetation. Once or twice a month, turn the compost well using a shovel or pitchfork. Doing so will redistribute the decomposing organisms, which tend to migrate towards the center of the pile. Add more organic material (carbon stuff and nitrogen stuff) as you acquire it.

If it's well-tended, a compost heap should be ready within 6 months. You can tell the heap is ready if it's dark, crumbly, and has a lovely fresh-earth smell.

NOTE: People disagree about whether or not to compost cat and dog poo. Carnivore feces can contain a lot of harmful bacteria that you don't want near edible plants. Because of this, most folks will tell you to keep any and all dog/cat/wolf shit far from your compost. However, some people argue that a very active compost heap can get hot enough to kill pathogens – 160°F, to be exact. So, if you want to compost pet waste, please make sure you've got a real rager of a compost pile going. Otherwise, toss your shit elsewhere.

About Seeds

Some plants are pretty easy to grow from seed: herbs, for example, are laid-back and will most likely sprout anywhere you plant them.

Other plants are more finicky and I'll discuss them a bit later. If you're shopping for seeds, ask around first to find out if other gardeners you know favor specific brands; most experienced gardeners will have one or two brands that they find to be the most consistent and affordable. You might also try buying the same type of seed from two different sources and comparing the results of each.

For a more grassroots approach (no pun intended), check out local farmers' markets and community gardens to see if there is a seed-swapping collective or seed library in your area.

When you're planting seeds, you can either stick them straight in the ground, or you can start growing them in a small, well-controlled environment until they are big enough to be transplanted. Which path you take depends a lot on where you live: if you have good soil and consistently good weather, or if your plants are going to live in containers, direct planting is no big deal. If your area tends to get random cold snaps and weird weather patterns, as mine does, you can give your little ones a fighting chance by making sure they are strong and healthy before you put them outside. As you get more experienced as a gardener, you'll begin to cultivate (again, no pun) a sense of what kind of care to give a specific seed.

★NOTE: Always read your seed packets - they provide important information about water, sun, etc.

Direct Planting

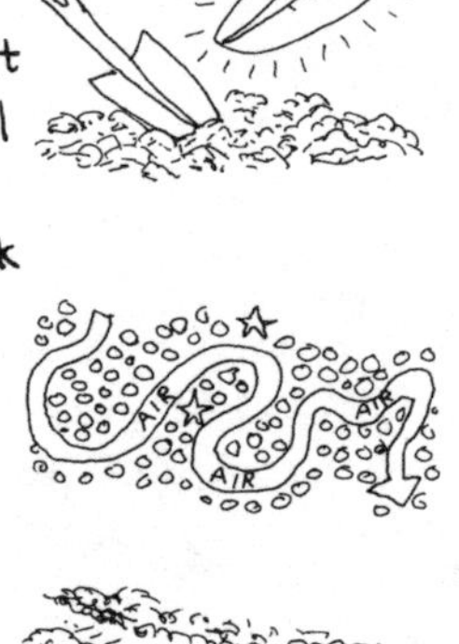

① Always prep your beds before you plant. The soil should be moist, but not wet – too much water will prevent air circulation in the soil. Use a trowel or shovel to turn over the first few inches of earth. Doing this helps break up clumpy or compacted dirt, and it introduces air into the soil, which improves drainage.

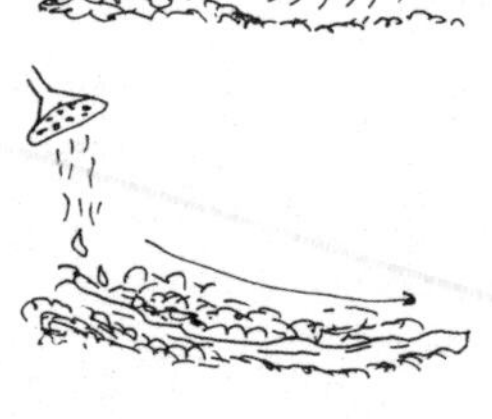

② After you've aerated, dig a little ditch with your trowel and shift the earth you dig out to one end of the ditch. It should look like a little slide. The depth and angle of the ditch will help direct and contain water. This is especially important if you have a diversity of plants in your garden, as some plants will need more water than others.

③ Sprinkle the seeds down into the ditch, not crowding them too much, and lightly cover them with soil. Small seeds (like herbs and lettuces) only need about 1/8" of soil on top. Bigger seeds will have to be planted farther down. Read your seed packet if you're unsure how deeply you should plant.

④ Finally, water your seeds and mark off your rows with sticks so you can tell where they are. You should also stick a label in there somewhere.

Ideas for recycled plant labels:

★ Cut a piece of clear or translucent plastic into strips or stake shapes and write on them with permanent marker. You can use milk bottles, salad bar clamshell containers, old blister packaging, or anything else you can think of. The translucency is important, as it will let light through to delicate seedlings.

★ Snip an aluminum can into strips and bend the strips around sticks or skewers. Write on the inside of the can by pressing hard on the metal with a ballpoint pen.

★ Save all your popsicle sticks, write on them with permanent marker or waterproof grease pencil, and cover with clear nail polish.

Growing Seedlings

Many gardeners prefer to start their seeds in a controlled environment until they develop into baby plants. You can do this with the help of some soilless seed starter and a lidless egg carton. You can use good potting or garden soil too, but since seed starting mix has no dirt in it, it's free of stuff like weed seeds and harmful bacteria. It also drains well.

Seed Starting Mix

You can find these ingredients at any nursery or hardware store:

1 part perlite

1 part peat moss

1 part ground sphagnum moss

Mix ingredients and keep in a bag or covered container, to keep out wayward seeds & spores.

If you don't feel like making starter mix, you can also use peat pellets, which you can buy for cheap at any nursery. Peat pellets are these amusing little pucks of peat moss that expand dramatically in water. They look like those little party favors that grow into wee face cloths with dinosaurs on them. But instead they turn into perfect little chunks of seed starter. Yippee!

+ 💧 = boop!

① Fill each depression with damp (but not wet) starter mix that you've loosened with your hands. Tamp the soil down lightly to firm it up a bit. If you're using pellets, soak them in water until they're fully expanded, and then put one pellet in each egg cup. Make a little dent in the center of each pellet.

yeah, I can't draw egg cartons. but you could use a muffin tin too! WHATEVER.

② Place a few seeds on each mound of dirt and cover the seeds lightly, or not so lightly, depending on the seed. Label your seeds, if you planted more than one kind.

③ Sprinkle the newly planted seeds with a little water.

④ If you like, cover the whole shebang loosely in clear plastic to create a tiny greenhouse. This will keep the seeds warm and moist. Keep the plastic on only until you see sprouts poking out. Also, make sure to let air circulate inside the plastic, to prevent molding.

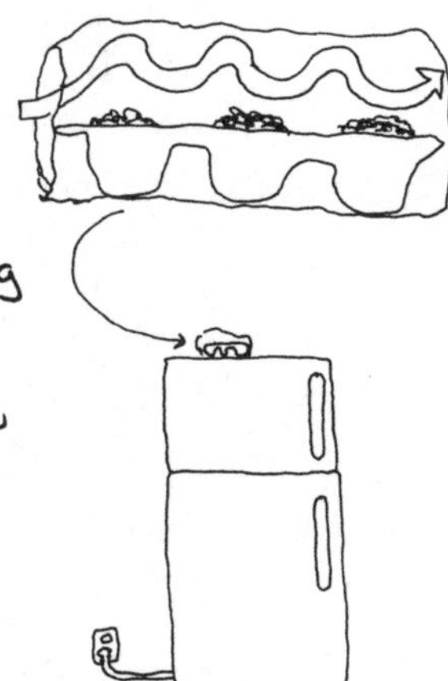

⑤ Place the egg carton in a warm spot and keep an eye on it. Since the seeds are still unsprouted, sunlight is not an issue, so don't bother putting them near a window.

⑥ Once you start to see signs of life, take the plastic off and move the carton into indirect light.

Take care of your plants until you can see that the new roots have reached the cardboard of the egg carton. From there, you can either transfer them to a bigger container that you've filled with garden or potting soil, or you can put them in the ground. But before you do either of those things, consider hardening off your plants. Maybe you are thinking, Ⓠ "what the hell is

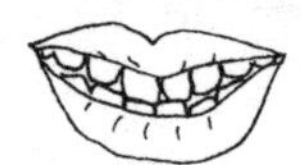

HARDENING OFF?"

Ⓐ This bizarre phrase refers to the process of gradually acclimating young plants to new growing conditions. It's sort of like getting your cat to eat a new kind of food- in order to not piss her off, you have to introduce the new stuff slowly until it is familiar and comfortable for her. If you have seedlings that you've been keeping indoors, or in a greenhouse, introduce them to the garden over a period of one or two weeks:

★ Begin to put your plants outside each morning. The first day, put them out only for a couple of hours; as the week progresses, leave them outside for longer and longer periods of time. You might also try switching periodically from sunny spots to shady spots.

★ Don't leave your babies at the mercy of the frosty night! If it's too cold, your plants won't get stronger— they'll just bite it. So bring them indoors or cover them if you think it's going to get chilly.

★ When you reach the point where you're leaving the seedlings out all the time, and they look strong and healthy, you can go ahead and transplant them to your garden (see "Planting Starts" on page 108). Try to transplant in the morning or evening, when the ground and air are not significantly hotter than the soil around the roots of the seedling. A smooth transplant means a healthier seedling!

Sprouting Seeds

If you're trying out a seed you've never planted before, or your seeds are from a new source, you'll want to sprout them first to make sure they are viable. Sprouting is easy and beautiful, and if you're sprouting beans or alfalfa, it's also quite delicious. I also recommend sprouting to anyone who's into plant morphology, because it allows you to witness a really amazing process that's usually hidden underground.

NOTE: Sprouting does take some finesse. Show your seeds some love!

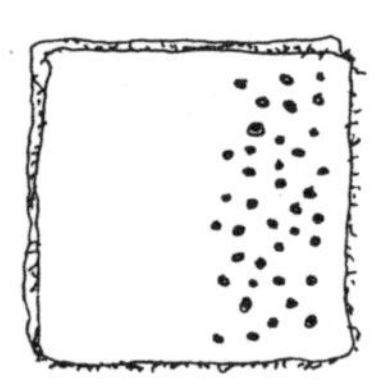

① On a tabletop or other flat surface, lay down two sheets of paper towel, one atop another. Sprinkle your seeds across one half of the resulting square.

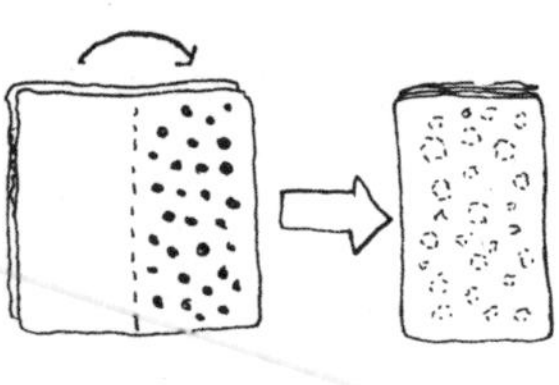

② Spread the seeds out in a single layer and fold the seed-free half of the towel over on top of the seeds.

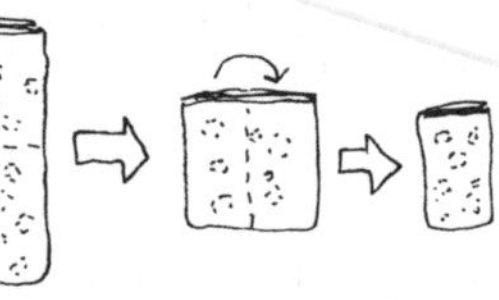

③ Fold the package twice more. Take care to keep the seeds from falling out or rolling around. This step should be done slooowly.

④ You should end up with a rectangle of towel about 8 layers thick. Add water to the towel a splash at a time, until all the layers are damp but not dripping wet. Try to get the towel to feel like a wet nap straight from the package.

⑤ Place the damp towel in a plastic bag, seal it up, and slap a label on it. If you accidentally over-wet your towel, leave the bag open to let it dry out a bit.

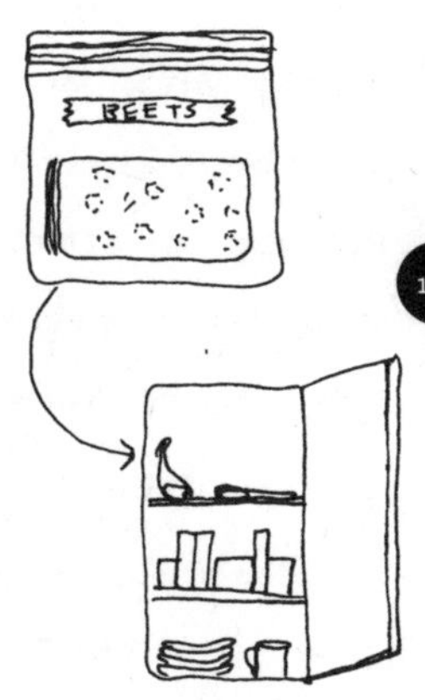

⑥ Let the sprouts sit in a cool place for about a week. Add water only if the towel is dried out; otherwise, give them their privacy. After a week is up, gently unfold the towel and- ta dah!- you've got a bunch of tittle squiggles that want planting.

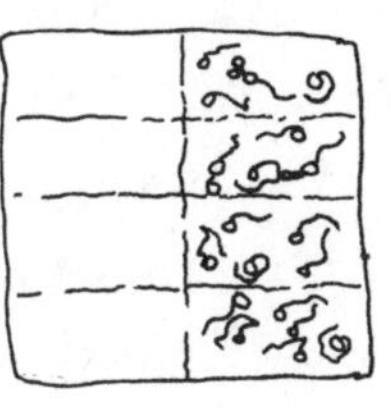

⑦ Very carefully remove sprouts from the towel and plant in the ground or in a seed starter medium.

Planting Starts

Some plants, like tomatoes, produce such delicate little seeds that a lot of gardeners don't even try to start from scratch. This is why most stores and markets you go to will have an abundance of small tomato plants (called starts) that are ready to be planted in the ground. A well-stocked nursery will have lots of different starts for vegetables, fruits, herbs, and ornamentals. Using a start relieves you of the burden of coaxing a seed to sprout and develop a root structure. If you've never grown anything before, taking care of a start will help you learn how plants develop and how to keep them healthy. Another plus: ♡instant gratification♡

① Prep your beds like you're planting seeds, then dig a hole that's a little deeper than you think it should be. You're looking to bury a little of the plant's shoot under the soil. This will encourage the plant to grow new roots at the soil line.

n

n+½"

② Fill the hole up with water. Gently remove the start from its little cup and look at it's lower half. You should find a compact ball of soil and roots. Loosen the root ball with your fingers, being careful not to tear or damage the roots.

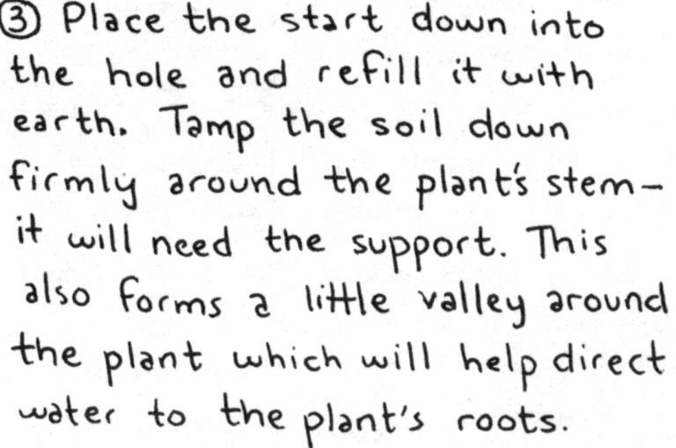

③ Place the start down into the hole and refill it with earth. Tamp the soil down firmly around the plant's stem– it will need the support. This also forms a little valley around the plant which will help direct water to the plant's roots.

When you're shopping around for starts, look for perky plants with sturdy main shoots, the thicker the better. Many lateral stems are also a good sign. Pass on plants that are super leggy*, are drooping over, or have signs of insect damage. If you like, you can hold the plant on its side and tug off the container to check the roots. Look for a root ball that's sizable, but does not make a tight basket around the inside of the container. Root-bound plants are difficult to transplant and will not grow very well.

* leggy = very long main shoot with few lateral stems

Watering

Misinformed watering is a really effective way to kill your plants. I feel like a lot of folks think that if they let their plants get dry their whole garden will, like, explode or melt or something. Ok, so nobody thinks that, but still, there's a lot of anxiety about the possibility of underwatering. The truth is that overwatering your plants can be just as bad for them, and damn wasteful to boot. So, here are some tips for proper watering:

- Water your plants whenever the soil is dry 1-3" below the surface, or if the plant looks withered. **Stick your finger** in the dirt to check dryness
- The best time to water is early morning or late afternoon. Daytime is just too hot - most of the water will just evaporate. Watering at night is usually ok, but it can sometimes put your plants at risk for mold.
- A thorough watering once or twice a week is almost always preferable to daily sprinkling. The exception to this is small seedlings, which need constant moisture. Watering deeply, but less often, will encourage plants to grow deep roots in order to search for moisture. Daily watering is unlikely to seep below the first few inches of soil, and the plants in turn will develop shallow, less stable roots.
- If you see flabby, yellowed leaves, you are overwatering.

fertilizing

I guess we'll call it the way of the civilized world: because vegetables as we know them have been cultivated for hundreds of years, most of them can no longer grow in regular garden soil. They're just used to being pampered. So even if you have naturally good soil and good seeds, you might need some fertilizer. Shopping for fertilizer is intimidating: you can choose either neon blue chemical powder or organic fertilizers like ground up fish. Both of these can seem bizarre and confusing to a novice gardener. Luckily, unless you have a very large operation underway, you won't have to deal with all that. There are lots of effective, sustainable fertilizers that can be had for next to no money. But first, some science.

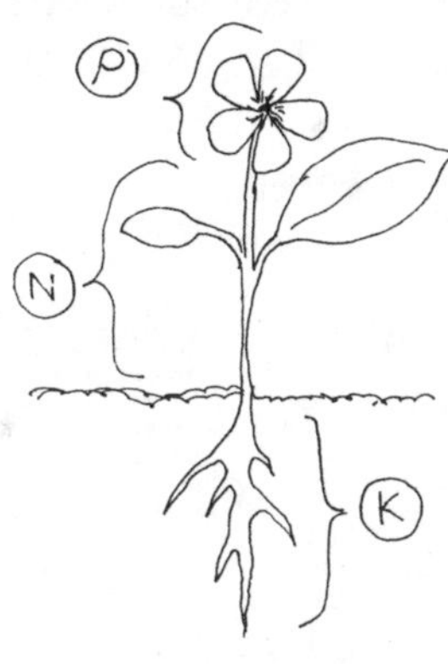

Plants need three main nutrients: nitrogen, phosphorous, + potassium. Nitrogen is essential in the formation of leaves and shoots, phosphorous encourages flowering, and potassium (potash) is a root stimulant. A good garden will need all three of these, plus a few trace nutrients like calcium and magnesium. Nitrogen, in its soluble form, is gobbled up by vegetables and is leached easily from the soil by rain or irrigation; if you live in a rainy climate or you water a lot, your garden might need a nitrogen boost more often. Other nutrients, especially potash + trace minerals, stick around a lot longer. Unless your garden is under constant torrential downpour (at which point an indoor garden is probably a good idea), you won't need to add these nutrients more than once or twice a year.

And now... we fertilize!

• Compost, your favorite thing in the world, is a fantastic fertilizer! Make sure your heap contains stuff like grass clippings, wood ashes, egg shells, used coffee grounds, and if you can get it, kelp and cow or horse manure. These materials make a very rich, balanced fertilizer. When your compost is totally decomposed, work it into your soil, a few pounds of compost per square foot of earth. This is best done in the fall when you're preparing your beds for winter, because the soil will settle over the cold months and the nutrients will be redistributed. Also make sure to put some 'post in the bottom of the holes you dig while transplanting seedlings or starts. You should also include a good amount of compost in any mix you're using to grow plants in containers.

A note about manure, and nitrogen in general: it might seem like a good idea to cut out the middleman and spread manure right on your beds, but it's really not. Manure and other really rich sources of nitrogen need to be aged and rotted through before they become usable, and that's why we compost them first. If you overfertilize by putting a buttload (pun totally intended) of manure on your beds, the nitrogen can actually scorch your plants. So, if you notice that the leaves in your garden look burned, even if they're not in direct sunlight, lay off the fertilizer, ok?

Manure tea: is easy to make. Just add a few handfuls of aged manure (available at nurseries) to a pail of water, let it sit around for an afternoon and use it to water new transplants or on plants that look wimpy, especially leafy greens.

Alfalfa tea: You can get alfalfa meal or pellets at the nursery. Put 10 or so double handfuls of alfalfa in a large, lidded container like a trash bin. Fill the bin mostly full of water, stir it with a big stick, lid it and leave it. Stir this once a day or so for 3-4 days or until it starts to smell truly disgusting. When that happens, it's ready! Scoop out some tea with a watering can and sprinkle onto soil that you've already irrigated with plain water. Keep your alfalfa tea in a sunny spot and keep it covered whenever you're not stirring. It really is nasty-smelling, but that goes away after awhile.

Staking & Trellising

If you're growing tomatoes, peppers, and the like, you're gonna need to overcome your fear of chicken wire (I know: it pokes!) and support those suckers. Viney plants like nightshades tend to have weak stems and heavy fruits. Once those fruits mature, they're liable to cause the plant to topple in bad weather and/or crush smaller plants. Plus, once the fruits are on the ground, the will most likely burst, rot, or invite hordes of crawling insects. To prevent this, support plant stems with a few stakes, or better yet, a cage. These are easy to make: just bend a rectangle of chicken wire (wear gloves!) into a cylinder and plop it over young plants. DONE!

Peas, beans and other vines need support too, but you've got tons more options:

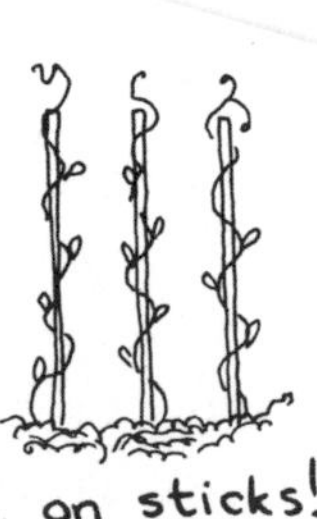

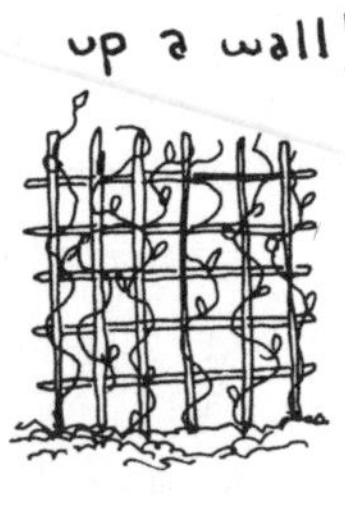

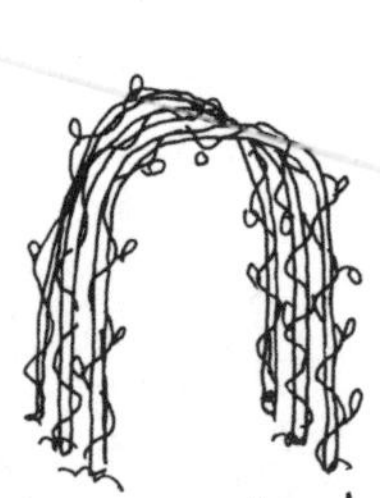

Vines climb stuff naturally, so to train peas and beans to grow on a support, you really just need to show them where it is. Young plants will start to sprout little tendrils that are quite strong: just wrap these early tendrils around your chosen support, and the vine will start growing up the support. Not only does this add a lovely vertical element to your garden, it makes peas and beans easier to pick! And bean tepees make the best forts ever.

★ If you have older* varieties of corn growing, try training pole beans to grow around the stalks! This is part of the "3 Sisters Garden" used by Native American tribes in the eastern part of North America. The other sister is squash, by the way. * older = stronger than newer hybrids

If you're gardening in a small space, try trellising other plants like squashes, cucumbers, raspberries, zucchini and eggplant. You can get creative here, just remember that a heavier plant will need a sturdier support. To keep fruits in place on the trellis, try securing the stems to the trellis with twine or cut-up pantyhose. Tie loosely to give the plant room to grow.

So, you've got leaves unfurling and your pea vines are spitting tendrils everywhere. Here is what to do to make sure your garden doesn't bite it:

Weeding

I know it sucks. I know it makes you uncomfortable to try and control what Nature graciously provides. But you gotta do it: if you don't, non-native noxious weeds will strangle your vegetables! *I am not kidding.* Keep your garden organized and you'll be able to spot young weeds and get them out before they produce seeds. If you can't get their roots out because they're too close to your veggies, cut them off at ground level and keep cutting them back until they're dead. And remember that a lot of weeds can be used medicinally, so once you get that plantain out of your garden, dry it and use it in a salve!

Thinning

As your vegetables come up, you'll probably have a few rows that are a little too crowded. Go over these rows and pick out a few of the scrawny-looking seedlings to give the healthy plants more room. Larger plants, like pumpkins and eggplants, will need more room between plants than, for example, snow peas. Plants won't grow if they don't have room, so give them their space!

Pruning - some plants, like tomatoes, ripen best in the sunshine. Snip off any leaves that are throwing shade over your fruits.

If you're growing herbs, they'll need to be pruned also. This will keep them growing outwards, rather than upwards. Pruning will also delay flowering, which can cause herb leaves to taste bitter. To trim plants, pinch off the tops of the stalks on a regular basis. They love it!

Preparing for Winter - Even if you planted a garden full of annuals, you'll probably be interested in keeping your soil viable until the next planting. There a couple of ways to do this.

① Start early and till your soil in the fall, after you harvest. Work in compost and other amendments, and cover with a layer of mulch to protect the topsoil.

② If you have any perennials planted, they'll live underground through the winter. Pick off any old stems or leaves on top of the soil, and add a layer of mulch to keep roots warm.

③ Plant a cover crop! A cover crop will maintain soil integrity, keep weeds from germinating, and, in the spring, it can be dug into the earth to enrich the soil. Grains like rye and winter wheat are popular cover crops. If you're a serious DIYer, you can even harvest your cover crop!

PEST CONTROL

Regardless of how urban your garden might be, it's still part of an ecosystem that includes bugs, deer, birds, and other animals that will enjoy eating the fruits of your labor. They're a royal pain, to be sure, but try to remember that these creatures are just doing what they do. Try not to take it personally! Instead of directing your malice towards them, try to control intruders without killing them. I think it's worth it, even though it's a bit more work. This section will focus on using preventative measures whenever possible, to keep pests out of your garden in the first place. Let's work big to small:

- Deer can usually be kept out with a good fence. You can either install a fence around your whole yard, or make a small garden enclosure out of chicken wire. You can also try gathering human hair clippings, stuffing them in the toes of some old nylons, and hanging them around the perimeter of their garden. Deer think you reek and will avoid anyplace that smells like people.

- Dig out a shallow trench and <u>then</u> install your fence, so part of it is underground; it will guard against rabbits. You can also try scattering human hair around your garden, placing a few vinegar-soaked corncobs in between plants, or sprinkling some red pepper flakes over the dirt. If you like bunnies but don't want them eating your lettuce, plant some clover in another part of your yard - it's one of their favorite foods.

• To keep cats from digging in your yard, take a few handfuls of thin sticks or skewers and stick them in the dirt at an angle. The sticks will make it so kitties won't be able to find a clear space to squat in. Two more ideas: ① Plant a border of lemon thyme or lemon balm (cats don't like citrus); ② divert their attention with a plot of catnip elsewhere in your yard.

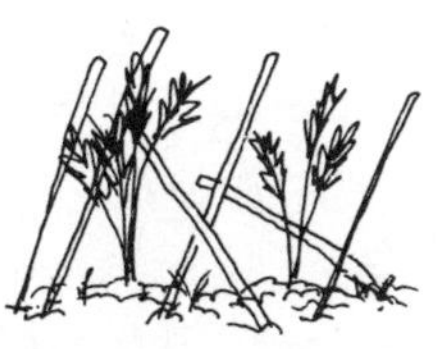

• Moles don't eat veggies, but they will uproot them in the course of their digging. To prevent this, plant vegetables in a raised bed, lined at the bottom with some wire mesh.

• Some light netting draped over vegetables (or arced over them with half hoops) will keep birds from eating fruits and scratching in the ground. A nice distracting birdfeeder can also help.

BUGS!

Alas, you cannot simply build a tiny fence to keep bugs out of your yard. But! There are some ways to control them without resorting to crop dusting. Specific bugs might need specialized care, but here are the basics:

• Know your bug before you launch an attack. A lot of insects are a) just minding their own and not actually hurting your garden, b) only there short-term and will happily leave on their own,

c) actually beneficial to your garden. Focus your energy on bugs that you know are hurting your plants, especially if they're non-native.

• A diverse, healthy garden will attract far fewer pests than an unkempt monoculture. Plant a lot of different veggies, don't overwater, and if your plants die, don't leave their corpses lying around.

• Attract beneficial bug-eaters, like ladybugs, praying mantis, green lacewings, and bats. You can also buy ladybugs and houses for bats. To attract ladybugs, plant umbrella-shaped plants like fennel, dill, and cilantro.

• Strong smelling plants like mint, garlic and rosemary will repel and confuse insects.

• If you find bugs on your plants, a strong spray from a hose will knock them off. Bigger ones (like slugs) can be picked off by hand and dropped into a bucket of soapy water (violent, I know. I'm sorry).

• Add a few tablespoons of castile soap (mint-scented, if you have it) to a gallon of water and pour some in a spray bottle. Spray on bugs you find on indoor or outdoor plants. Make sure you rinse veggies before you eat them!

• Plant a row of sacrificial plants (radishes are good) around your garden to distract bugs from more precious crops

this here's a pot!

indoor + container gardening

I'm going to assume that some of you out there are, like me, apartment dwellers. It has been years since I had my own yard; I spend a lot of time daydreaming about hammocks. Limited outdoor space is a part of the urban landscape - but that doesn't mean it should keep you from growing food! Luckily, container gardening is an option for almost everyone, and tons of fruits + veggies grow well in containers. Witness the ABUNDANCE!:

lettuces
beets
garlic
cabbage
peppers
strawberries
spring onions
tomatoes
carrots
radishes
herbs
anything that says "dwarf," "bush" or "compact" on the label

And now, the basics: you need a pot. Does it need to be a nice pot, or even a pot-shaped pot? Hell no! Pretty much any container that can hold soil, not rot away, and drain excess water can function as a planter. Depending on what plant you're growing, coffee cans, baskets, windowboxes, old boots, wooden crates, buckets, jugs and big sacks can all be utilized, as well as a host of other junk. Just make sure you can put at least two ½" drainage holes in the bottom. Also, choose a bigger container than you think you'll need - it needs to be big enough to accomodate a mature root system and wide enough so that the weight of the plant won't cause it to topple. Once you've got a sufficient container, line the base with newspaper to prevent soil erosion.

Secondly, dirt. Commercial potting soil is usually made of peat and other light, quick-draining stuff. These materials are weed- and disease-free, and they keep plants from getting waterlogged. The DIY version of potting soil is compost, or compost mixed with a bit of sand - check your seed packets to see if your seeds like sand in their soil. You yardless folks- check your local community garden to see if you can score some free compost.

Seeds for container gardens can be sprouted first or planted directly in their new home. Once you have some leaves sprouting, move the pot (or whatever) to the sunniest part of your house. Fruiting plants, like tomatoes, are especially greedy for sun. If you find that the sunniest part of your home = too much sun, you can move them. Because pots are awesome.

Since potting soil drains so quickly, container gardens need to be watered and fertilized more often than in-ground gardens. Water whenever the soil is dry under the surface, but not if only the first ½ inch or so is dry. If your plants need a boost, give them manure tea once in a while.

Resources and further reading

♡= favorites

General Herbal Health & First Aid

The Green Pharmacy, by James A Duke, PhD (Rodale Books, 1999)

♡The Backyard Medicine Chest, by Douglas Schar (Elliot & Clark, 1995) ♡

Prescription for Nutritional Healing, by Phyllis Balch (Avery, 2006)

♡Cat's Claw♡Herbal, by Heron (self-published)*

Herbal Gynecology

♡Hot Pantz:♡Do it Yourself Gynecology, by Isabelle Gauthier and Lisa Vinebaum (self-published)*

Take Back Your Life: A Wimmin's Guide to Alternative Health Care, by Alicia non Grata (Originally published by Profane Existence Collective)*

Nontoxic Cleaning and Body Care

♡Better Basics for the Home, b♡y Annie Berthold-Bond (Three Rivers Press, 1999)

The Naturally Clean Home, by Karyn Siegel Maier (Storey Publishing LLC, 1999)

Herbal Homekeeping, by Sandy Maine (Interweave Press, 1999)

*Available from Microcosm, www.microcosmpublishing.com

Clean House Clean Planet, by Karen Logan (Pocket, 1997)

Vim and Vinegar!, by Melodie Moore (Harper Paperbacks, 1997)

Baking Soda Bonanza!, by Peter E. Ciullo (Harper Perennial, 1995)

Gardening

♡ Compost This Zine, by Liz Defiance (self-published)

♡ Home Composting Made Easy (self-published)*

Basic Gardening, by Louise Carter (Fulcrum Publishing, 1995)

The Organic Suburbanite, by Warren Schultz (Rodale Books, 2001)

Dave's Garden - www.davesgarden.com

-A very active online community with tons of articles about all types of gardening

All Around DIY Amazingness

♡ Making Stuff and Doing Things, collected by Kyle Bravo (Microcosm Publishing, 2005)

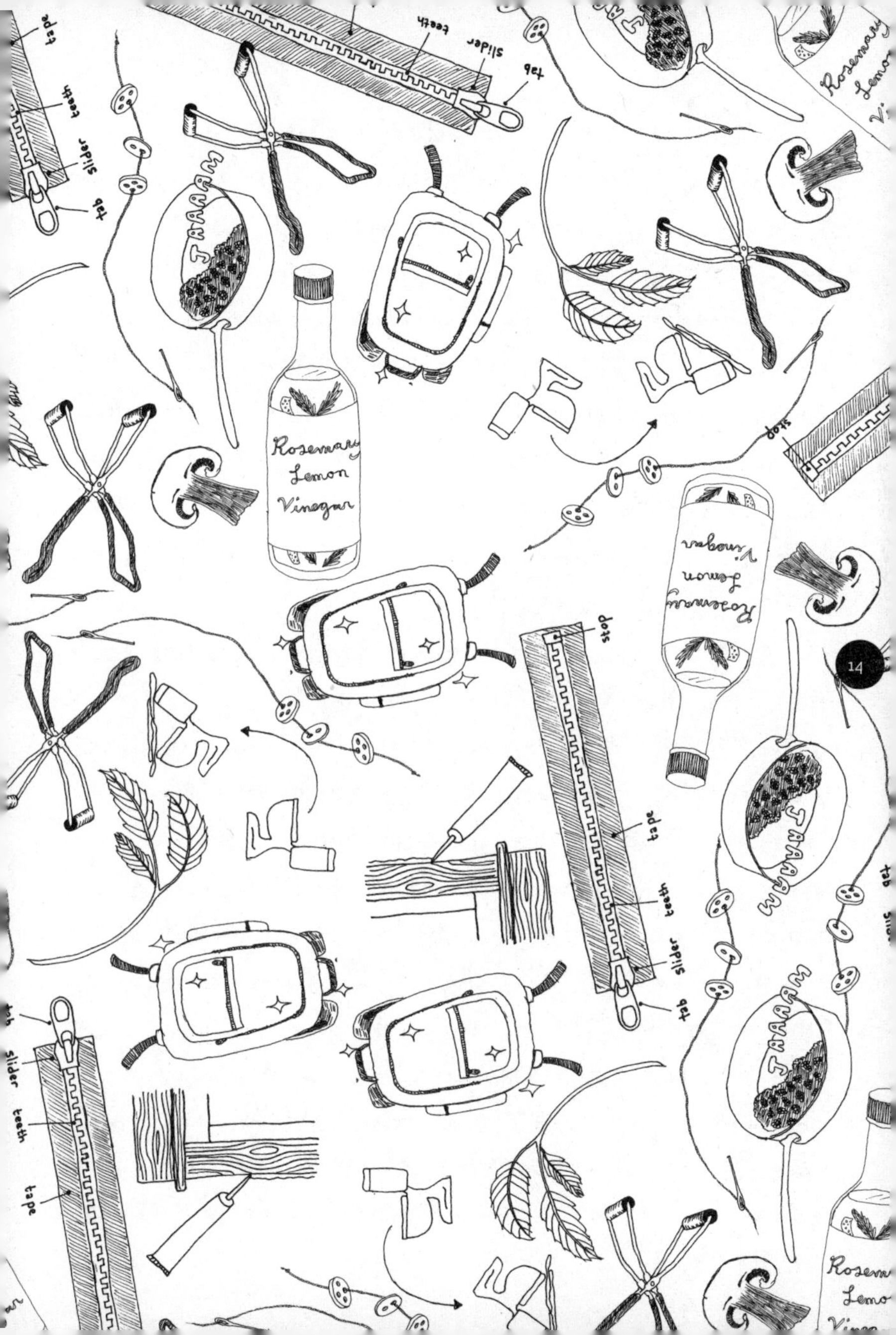
tape
teeth
slider
tab
stop
TAAAAM
Rosemary
Lemon
Vinegar
14

Hello, beautiful readers. Thank you for picking up this new edition of Make It Last! It's been a decade plus since I wrote this book, and so much has changed in my life, and in the world. As I write this in 2024, we citizens of Earth are enmeshed in a cycle of waste and exploitation that goes far beyond our choices as individual consumers. Late-stage capitalism is a serious drag, and unfortunately learning to mend and pickle is not going to make it go away.

But that doesn't mean these acts of love and care don't matter—I would say they matter more than ever. Humans need connection and creation to survive. We connect when we pass on what we no longer need, and when we share our skills with each other. And when we prolong the life of a useful object, that is an act of creation. The object becomes something new when we imbue it with our energy and knowledge. Yes, it's practical, and often necessary. But it's also magical! And so very important. I hope you get good use out of this book. It is an honor to connect and create with you. ♡

~INTRODUCTION~

Over the past few years, American culture has seen a big swing toward the sustainable, the home-grown, and the self-maintainable. What's even more incredible is that traditional skills like canning are being picked up by tons of different communities, from young professionals to radical collectives—and this is in addition to the rural and working-class folks who have been doing this stuff for generations. Can you remember the last time so many people were into the same thing? (Was it Justin Timberlake?) I don't know, but it's amazing.

It's hard to ignore the energy and momentum of the movement toward making or repairing things instead of buying them. It's not a giant revolution (yet), but for those of us who can afford to buy interminable versions of the same products, it represents a huge paradigm shift. Choosing to preserve is about realizing that the planned obsolescence and semi-disposability built into today's consumer goods are part of a marketing plan. They're not unavoidable facts of life. It's convenient for a manufacturer to sell a $5 shirt with buttons that pop right off after two washes.

But it's not convenient for us, and we don't have to put up with it if we don't want to.

That's why this book is devoted to the art and science of preservation. We'll focus on clothing, food, and home repair, but if you like this stuff, why stop there? Learn to fix your car or your bike. Take a soldering class. The possibilities are endless! Preservation makes great economic and environmental sense, and unlike some of the more intensive DIY disciplines, it's available to everyone—even if you don't have time, space, or resources to sew clothes, grow food, or build stuff, you can take the clothes, food, and, uh, built stuff that you have and make them last longer. People are starting to realize not only that they <u>can</u> do this stuff, but that it's fun and fulfilling, to boot.

Since writing <u>Make Your Place</u> four years ago, I've had the unique experience of getting to know lots of people who want to explore DIY and add to their own skill set. It's been so inspiring to hear how resourceful, creative, and smart people are. I'm looking forward to hearing about the ingenious repairs you'll make around your own abodes. So please, enjoy <u>Make It Last</u>, and keep those emails coming. (I got a new address just for you: raleigh.briggs@gmail.com)

P.S.! Whenever I'm exhibiting, a reader always approaches me and says something like, "I was running home and I realized we didn't have any laundry soap so I bought some instead of making it. I AM SO SORRY!" They apologize to me! I want to address that here, because it's so sad that people would think I would judge them because they bought soap for their family. Listen: DIY and self-righteousness have a long history together. There will always be people who are going for the gold in the DIY Olympics. But please: The goal is not to ever buy anything so you can achieve some mythical perfection. At some point in your life, you're going to buy a shirt instead of fixing an old one. That is fine! Whenever you think about the choices you're making, you're doing a good thing. So do what you can, and don't stress.

~ I believe in you. ~

chapter 4

CLOTHES

In this first chapter, we'll be talking about clothes. Unless you wear seamless, zipperless, indestructible coveralls (email me if you do!), you've had to deal with the fact that clothes are mortal. We love them, but they fail us in myriad ways. Whether you buy new or used clothing, you have to deal with the seam that busts when you bend over. The zipper that slips down to reveal your underpants to your coworkers. The cute and cheap outfit that turns out to be just ... cheap.

All of these things are annoying, but none of them have to ruin your day. Even if you haven't sewn so much as a pillowcase, it's worth your time to learn a few basic clothing repairs. You don't have to buy new jeans every time the inner thighs wear out—just patch them up and keep rocking them! You'll save money, save those jeans from premature death in some landfill, and create something that is, in its own humble way, uniquely yours. Your first few projects might look goofy, it's true, but they'll still look better than giant holes in your clothes. So let's get started.

SUPPLIES

Just a few little things you'll need before you start sewing:

Needles

A good multipack of needles can get you through most DIY fixes. You'll need some thin needles (for delicate fabrics) and a few thicker ones for mending denim or canvas.

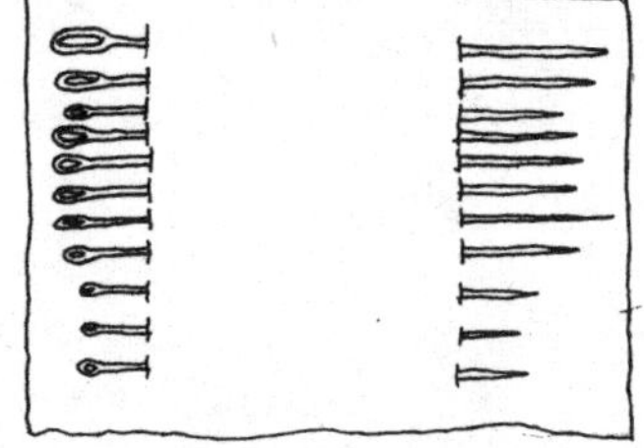

Thimble

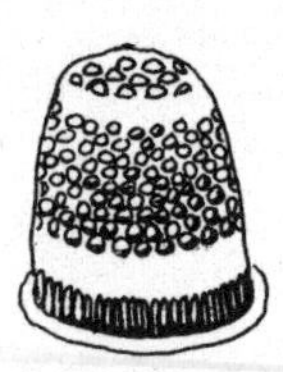

If you think you don't need a thimble, just try to hem some jeans without crying.

Thread

If you're just beginning to sew, the thread section of the fabric store can induce a feeling of "thread panic," a term I just made up. Thread comes in all different thicknesses, colors, and fibers, and it can be hard to know what to pick for your project.

If you're just doing basic mending and alteration, you should be fine with just a couple of spools. Cotton-wrapped polyester thread will give you the most versatility for your buck. It's strong, heat-resistant, and will work on most fabrics. Get a spool each of white, black, and whatever color is most dominant in your wardrobe.

Seam Ripper

The sharp mandibles of a seam ripper undo stitches gracefully, without tugging. Use the blunt-tip side to loosen a stitch, then flip the ripper over and use the sharp prong to cut the thread.

Measuring Tape + Ruler

The fancy clear rulers are especially nice for sewing. Any tape measure will do as long as it's flexible.

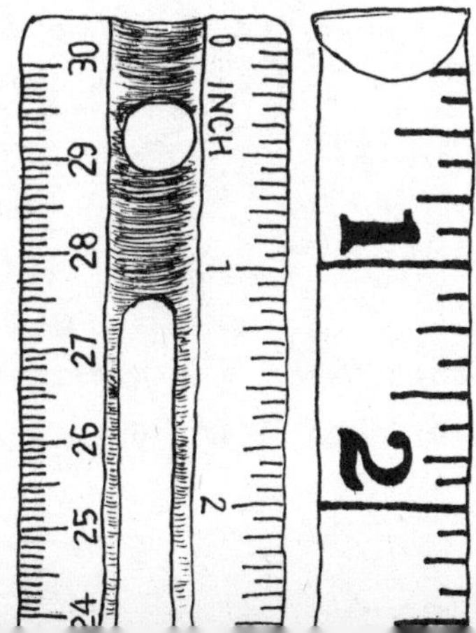

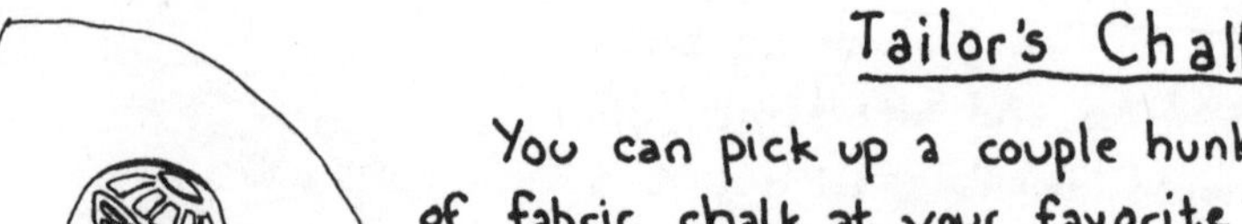

Tailor's Chalk

You can pick up a couple hunks of fabric chalk at your favorite craft store. Some of them even come with little brushes that erase the marks when you're done. If chalk's not your thing, you can also find markers that wash out.

Notions

These will depend on what sorts of clothes you like to wear, but a well-stocked notions stash usually contains two- and four-hole buttons, hook & eye sets, zippers, snaps, and patches.

Beeswax

Folks who hand-sew use beeswax to add strength and glide to their thread. To do this, hold one end of your thread against the wax, with your finger a couple inches from the thread's tip. Grab the short end of the thread with your other hand and pull the whole length of the thread across the wax. (Most commercial waxes have holders with little guides to keep the thread from slipping off.) Do this a couple times so that the thread is nicely coated.

Next, run over your thread with a warm iron to melt the wax into the thread. This might seem fussy, but the ironing is important—it removes any waxy residue and creates a strong, tangle-free thread with plenty of glide.

Pins & A Pincushion

Buy a tin of straight pins with the little pearls on the ends. Keeping a couple dozen in a pincushion will keep you from having to pull a single pin from a pile of bloodthirsty ones.

Fabric Scissors

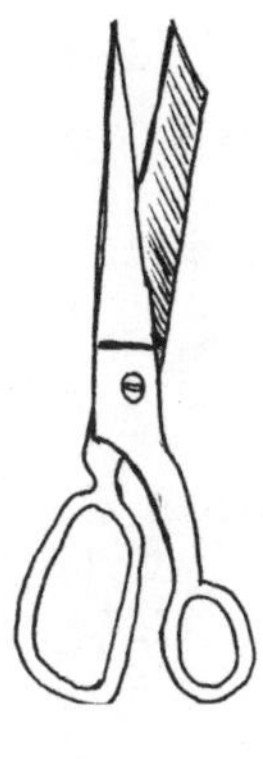

A modest but decent-quality pair is all you need. You needn't spend tons of money, but if you want your scissors to stay sharp, avoid using them to cut anything other than fabric. Paper, plastic, or cardboard can make the blades too blunt.

Quick Fixes!

Sometimes you absolutely don't have time to sew on a button, and that's okay. Walking around with buttonless pants, however, is probably not okay. You can avoid these little mishaps by creating an emergency mending kit, filled with McGyver-y supplies to hold you over until you can do some real mending. Reach for it next time your (totally hypothetical) jeans button pops off post-breakfast burrito and it's making you late for work.

A few things to add to your kit:

* safety pins for popped buttons + "librarian's gaps"
* Fray Check (a liquid plastic that stops fabric from fraying)
* Iron-on hemming tape or double-sided tape
* a few cute pins or pin-on buttons (for strategic stain coverage)
* a mini-stapler, for VERY quick n'dirty hem fixes

Basic Knots + Stitches

Knots! And stitches! You need to learn a few of them. But don't be nervous. Hand-sewing does require a bit of motor skill, but mostly it requires you to be patient, or at least to have a good movie to watch while you're working. The fineness and evenness of your stitches will improve with practice, so jump right in!

If you already sew a bit, feel free to skip ahead. If you're a newbie, here are some basic stitches you should learn.

Starter's Knot

Every sewing project starts with a single knot. Beginning sewers tend to make their knots really big, hoping this will keep the knot from pulling through the fabric. But a big knot can get tangled in your other stitches. It also uses a bunch of thread that can be put to better use elsewhere. Also it looks weird!

So save yourself the trouble and keep your knot simple. Make a slipknot at the end of your thread. Take the needle through the loop and pull the rest of the thread through. Then, pinch the whole shebang between your thumb and forefinger, and slide the knot to the end of the thread until it's tight.

Tying Off

Again, don't waste your time tying tons of knots to secure your work. To make a knot that lies flat and doesn't bunch, first bring your thread and needle to the wrong side of the thread. Make a tiny stitch that's perpendicular to your other stitches, pull the thread most of the way through, then take your needle under the thread that's left. Pull the thread tight-ish and repeat with another stitch. Make sure your thread is secure, then snip the thread to ½ inch.

KNOW YOUR KNOTS + STITCHES

starter knot

tying off

straight stitch

basting stitch

blanket stitch

backstitch

overhand stitch

slipstitch

Straight Stitch

Use it to: join two pieces of fabric; make simple hems; gather fabric

As basic as it gets! Thread your needle, make a knot at one end, and push the needle from the wrong side to the right side of the fabric. Then, use your needle to weave through the fabric in a straight line, creating a few stitches. Try to keep your stitches even. Pull your thread through (try not to bunch the fabric) and repeat as needed.

Basting Stitch

Use it to: hold your fabric in place while you're sewing—like straight pins, but less pokey

A basting stitch is pretty much a long, loose straight stitch. When you baste, use a thread in a contrasting color so that you can easily find and remove the stitches later.

Blanket Stitch

Use it to: make a decorative edging; attach two pieces of fabric along their edges

Thread your needle and take it from wrong to right side through the edge of the garment so that the needle comes out the bottom.

Take the needle over the edge of the fabric (so it's behind the fabric again) and bring it through again at a point a little ways over and above from where you brought the thread through the first time. Move your needle so that it's inside the loop formed by the stitch you just made, and pull the thread through. If you're right-handed, you'll see that the stitch forms a backwards L. Lefties will see a regular L. Make another stitch by taking your needle over the edge to the back of the fabric, coming through to the front, catching the needle, and pulling through.

Backstitch

Use it to: mend seams; replace zippers

Backstitching gives you a tight, strong line without any gaps, so it's great for decorative stitching, too. A caveat: backstitching looks crappy from the wrong side of the fabric, so don't use it on anything that needs to be reversible.

To create a backstitch, start like you're making a straight stitch. Bring your needle up as if you're making a second stitch, but instead of bringing your needle forward along the seam you're making, bring the needle back about a half stitch's length and insert your needle through the middle of the stitch to the back of the fabric. Angle your needle forward and bring the tip to the front about a half stitch's length in front of where you first brought the thread through. Pull the needle and thread through all the way.

Make the next stitch by bringing the point of your needle backwards again and inserting it from front to back at the halfway mark of your first stitch. Again, angle your needle forward and bring the point to the front a half stitch ahead of your last stitch. Pull everything through and continue like this until you're done.

Overhand Stitch/Whipstitch

Use it to: finish an edge; create a buttonhole

An overhand stitch is done over the edge of your fabric, rather than parallel to an edge. Bring your needle up through the fabric about ¼ inch from the edge, then wrap it around the fabric's edge and back to the wrong side. Bring your needle up again in a spot that's very close to your previous stitch and pull the thread through. This way you'll create a tight row of stitches that "seal" the edge of the fabric in thread.

Slipstitch

Use it to: create an invisible hem

A very classy stitch that's great for making hems in delicate or fancy clothes. To make a slip-stitch, start by holding your basted hem horizontally. Slip your thread under one or two threads from the outer fabric (the part that's not folded), and then, moving forward a little along the hem, pick up two threads from the folded portion of the hem. Head back up to the outer fabric, create a teeny stitch like before, then repeat with the inner fabric. Continue making this delicate little zigzag until your hem is complete.

TIP!: Are you having trouble making a straight line? You can use a ruler and tailor's chalk to create a guide before you start sewing.

BUTTONS

Even if you don't plan on ever making your own clothes, it's imperative that you learn how to sew on a button. Because inevitably, there will come a time when a missing button is what keeps you from wearing your favorite interview skirt, cardigan, catsuit, or whatever. Sure, a safety pin will do in a pinch, but *come on.*

Let's sew buttons!

Flat Buttons

If your button's destiny is to close a shirt, secure a pocket, or just look pretty, a flat button will do the trick.

Step 1: Grab your garment, a button, a needle, and six inches of thread. If you're picky, make sure to choose thread that matches the thread used on the other buttons. Pick a thin needle that can easily fit into the holes of the button.

Step 2: Cut 6-10 inches of thread. Wax your thread if you like (see page 8). Thread the needle and pull half the thread through. Then, use an overhand knot to tie the ends of the thread together.

Step 3: Pick where you'd like to place your button.

Step 4: Insert the needle into the fabric on the wrong side (the side that faces in toward your body). Pop the button on top and pull the needle through.

Step 5: Go back down through the opposite hole you came up through. Repeat! Repeat 4 or 5 times more.

Step 6: If your button has four holes, repeat steps 4 and 5 on the other two holes. End with your needle on the wrong side of the fabric and the thread pulled all the way through.

Step 7: Tie an overhand knot in the thread, as close to the fabric as you can get. Snip the thread. You're all done!

Shank Buttons

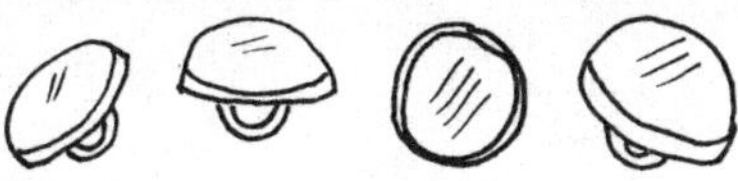

If your garment is made of thicker material (like denim or canvas), you should use a shank button. Instead of holes in its face, a shank button has a raised area or loop on the back. Shank buttons are also used for the flies of pants and other *high-stress* areas (heh).

When you're placing or replacing a shank button, upgrade from all-purpose to quilting thread—it's a lot stronger and comes in a billion colors, just like all-purpose.

Step 1: Start with about 2 feet of thread, a thickish needle, beeswax (if using), a thimble, and a small, clear button (optional).

Step 2: Wax your thread (extra important if you're using all-purpose thread instead of something stronger). Thread your needle, pull half of the thread through, and knot both ends of the thread together, creating a strong double thread.

Step 3: Choose where you will place your button and bring the needle up from the wrong side of the fabric. Make a few small stitches over your chosen spot before you add the button.

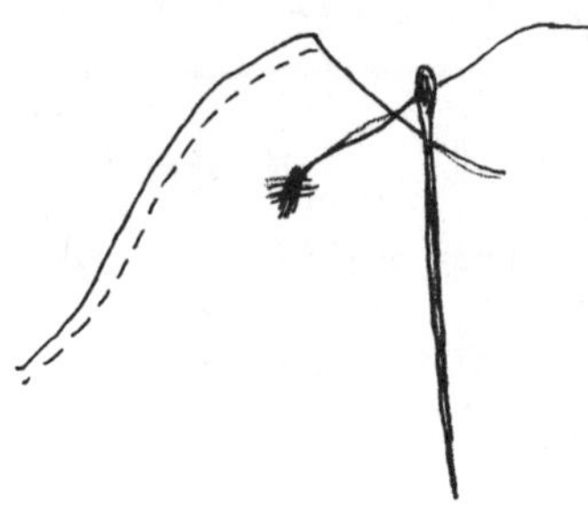

Step 4: Place the small, clear button on the inside of the garment, on top of the stitches you just made. Anchor this button with a few stitches. This will help add stability to your shank button and cut down on fabric wear later on.

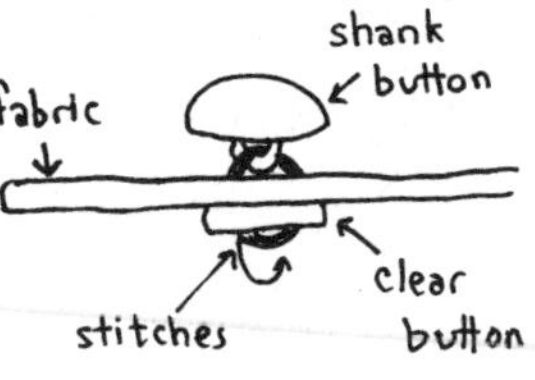

Step 5: Hold your shank button in place on the outside of the garment and tack it in place with a few semi-tight stitches. Make sure you're sewing these same stitches in the clear button on the other side.

NOTE: Don't pull your thread tight when you make these stitches. If you can't help it, slide a toothpick under the button's shank while you stitch.

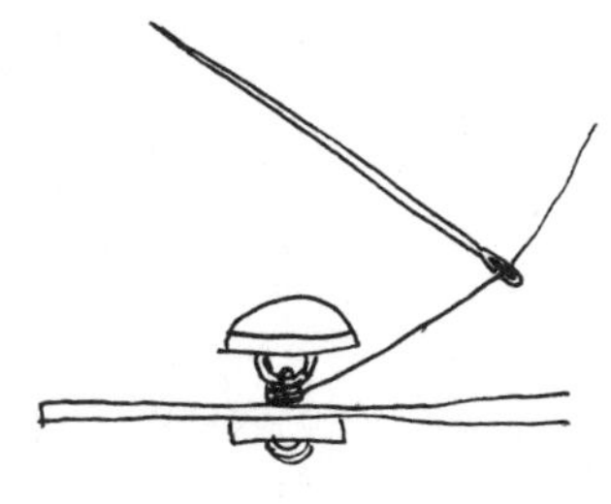

Step 6: After you have 5 or 6 stitches holding your buttons in place, pull the needle one more time to the fabric's right side, then wrap the thread around the stitches holding the shank in place. Do this several times.

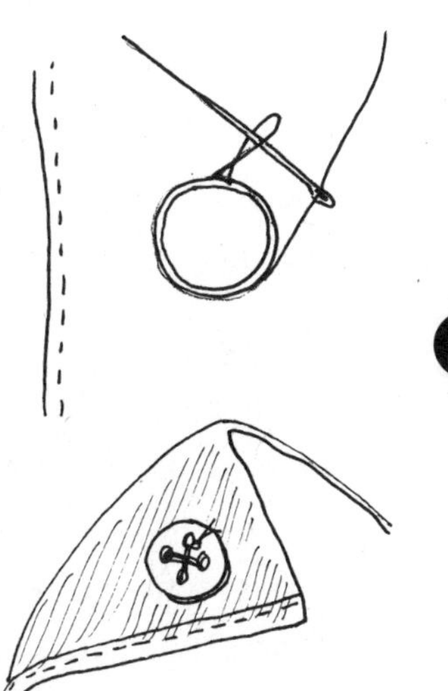

Step 7: Make a teeny loop in the thread on the needle; hold it with a finger. Bring the needle around the shank and through the loop, then pull the thread tight. Repeat this a few times.

Step 8: Finally, bring your needle back to the wrong side, knot off + snip your thread.

TIPS! A lot of garments come with a spare button, either in a baggie or stitched into the garment in an inconspicuous place. Before you buy new buttons, check the tails and insides for a spare.

Also, when you spill ink on a shirt or its armpits rot out, cut off all the buttons before you scrap it. Now you have a free set of buttons. You're welcome!

Mending Seams

If you could choose a way for your clothes to break, you'd pick a busted seam. Fixing a seam is a piece of cake! The pieces of fabric are already lined up and held in place by the stitches that didn't bust, and most of the time you don't have to deal with damaged fabric. Seams are easy to fix even if you're not the world's greatest stitcher, so don't be intimidated by the prospect of having to sew in a straight line.

Prep

First things first! Check out your seam. Did the seam tear because the thread holding it together broke or because the fabric around the seam was too damaged to hold? If you're dealing with torn or damaged fabric, skip ahead to the section on patching. You'll need to patch over the missing bits first and then incorporate that fabric into your seam.

No damage? Sweet. Use a double knot to tie off the threads on either side of your open seam. The knot should be snug, but not so tight that it causes the rest of the seam to bunch up.

Trim the ends of the knots so that they don't poke through to the other side. This is important: A seam with uneven stitches can still pass as charming; a seam with squiggly threads poking out just looks dumb.

Press

If you have time, press your seam open before you start mending. This will help you keep track of your seam allowances (the distance between the seam and the fabric's edge) and give you a neat, perfect seam. If you don't care about looking perfect, I don't blame you. Read on.

Pin

Even if you're in a hurry, *please* don't forget to pin your seam before you start sewing. I can't stress this enough! Pins will keep the fabric together so you can concentrate on sewing a straight line and keeping your stitches even.

To pin, turn your garment inside out (if you hadn't already), find the busted part of the seam, and line up the edges of the fabric. Bridge the gap in the seam by placing pins perpendicular to the edge of the fabric, tips pointing out.

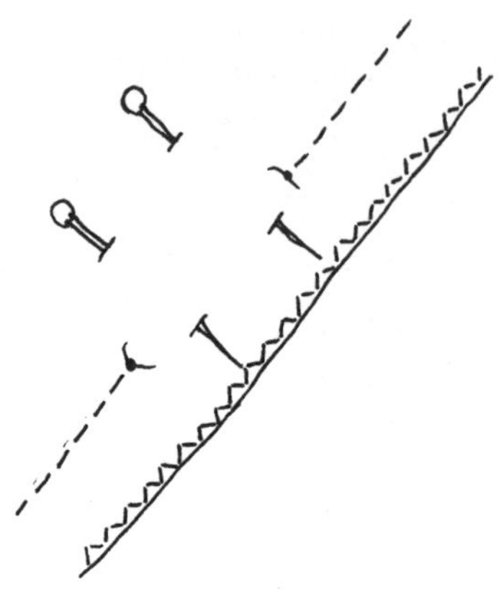

What? You're in a hurry AND all your pins fell into the toilet? Use clear or masking tape folded over both edges of the fabric.

Stitch

Begin your stitching about 3/4 inch before the missing part of the seam to ensure there won't be a gap between the old seam and your new one.

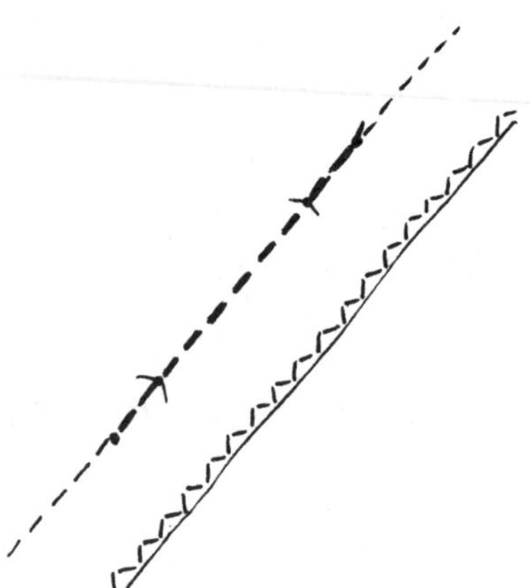

Then, just stitch a new seam where the old seam was. Use the holes of the old seam as a guide. Remove your pins as you work.

Use a backstitch or small straight stitches—whatever fits closest with the rest of the seam. Sew about 3/4 inch beyond the gap on the other end, then knot and snip your thread.

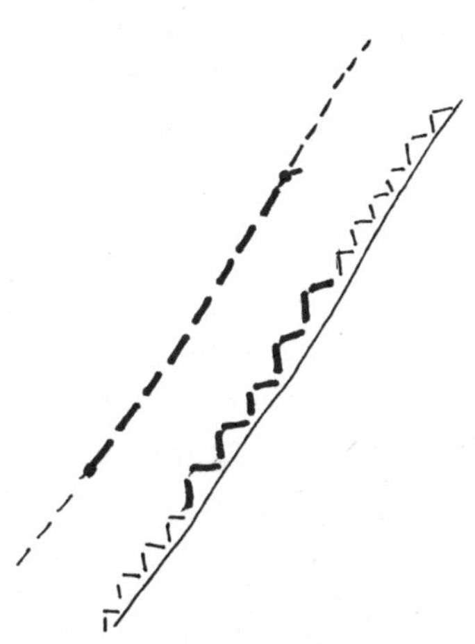

Finish

Check the edge of your fabric. Is it finished with a zigzag or overhand stitch? If so, did these stitches come undone when your seam ripped? Keeping those edges unfinished can leave your fabric vulnerable to fraying.

If you have the time, replacing those finishing stitches with a quick zigzag or overhand stitch of your own will keep the fabric from unravelling. There's no sense in mending a seam just to fix it again when the fabric unravels!

P.S., you can also treat a fabric's edges with a drop or two of Fray Check, which you can find at the fabric store.

PATCHING HOLES

Torn or worn-through fabric is a different mending experience than, say, an unravelled seam. Because a hole can weaken the fabric around it, you can't just sew it up with a row of stitches. Instead, you have two options: patch it or darn it. Sewing on a patch is often preferable to darning the hole itself.

DO NOT be seduced by the lure of the iron-on patch! Iron-ons might seem easy, but the adhesive is always jacked, and your fabric + color choices are depressing. Patching is an art form, and those tan drugstore patches are the equivalent of Thomas Kinkade paintings. Avoid at all costs!

When you choose a patch, find a fabric that's similar to that of what you're mending. Match exactly if you can, but at least find something with a similar weight and stretch. As for color, that's really up to you! If you want an exact match, you can use fabric from the garment itself to patch the hole. Just sew up a seldom-used pocket (such as the back or coin pockets in a pair of jeans,) and cut a little fabric away from the layer underneath the pocket.

HOW TO PATCH The Fancy Way

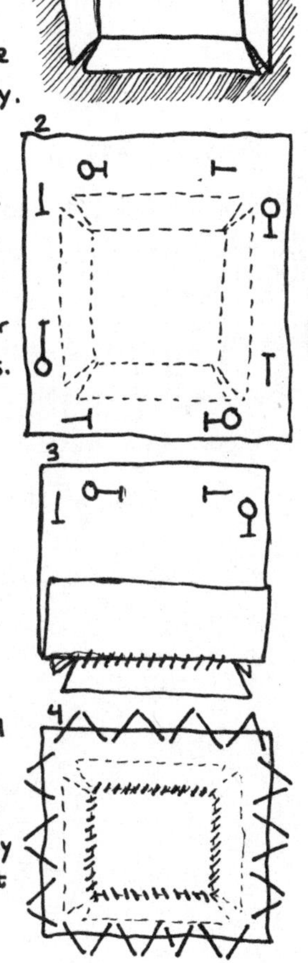

Step 1: Trim away the fabric around the hole until it's a nice square. Snip a 1/4 inch slit in each corner and fold these flaps inside the garment so it forms a "frame" around the hole on the wrong side of the fabric. Iron these flaps so they stay.

Step 2: Cut enough patch fabric to extend at least 1/2 inch beyond the hole on all sides. If your patch and garment are printed, align them in a way that looks good to you. Iron the patch and pin it over the hole, matching the grain of the fabrics. Try not to stretch or bunch the fabric. You can also baste the patch in place.

Step 3: Thread your needle with a double length of thread and tie the ends together. Fold back the extra 1/2 inch of patch fabric on one side, and using tiny diagonal stitches, sew the fold of the patch fabric to the folded edge of the garment fabric. Stitch all the way around the hole + knot off.

Step 4: Finish by tacking down the edges of the patch with little zigzag stitches. Only pick up a few threads with each stitch. Knot off and snip any loose threads. Done!

HOW TO PATCH THE QUICK & DIRTY WAY

AKA the punk-patch special. Who needs hidden stitches?

Step 1: Snip any loose or hanging threads from around the hole. Pin on your patch, matching the grain of the fabrics. Try not to bunch or stretch the fabric, if you can help it.

Step 2: Thread your needle with a double length of thread and tie the ends together. Start at one corner of the patch and bring your needle up from underneath. From there, stich around all the edges of the patch using either diagonal stitches or blanket stitches. Try to keep your stitches even and loose enough to not tug on the patch fabric. End with your needle on the wrong side of the fabric and knot off. Done done done

1

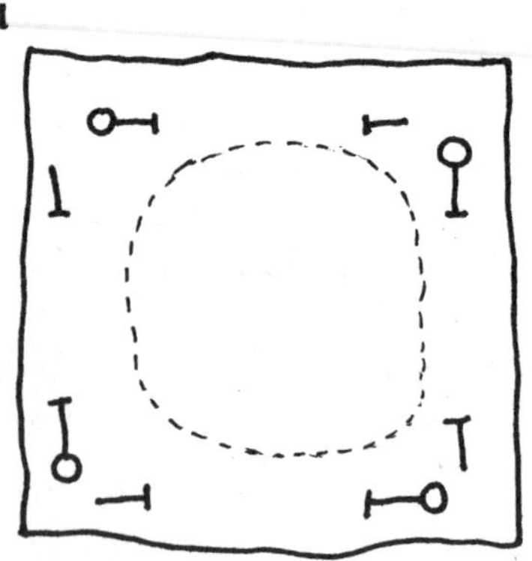

2

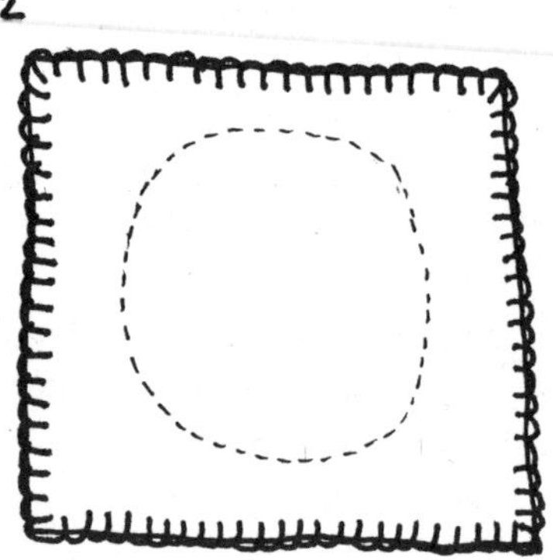

Darning Holes

What, you're not satisfied with just slapping a patch on your pants and calling it a day? You want to actually *fix* the hole? WELL FINE.

When you darn a hole, you're using thread to weave a tiny bit of cloth to replace what's been lost. This is a little tedious to accomplish, but if you want to keep wearing that favorite pair of socks, it's totally worth it.

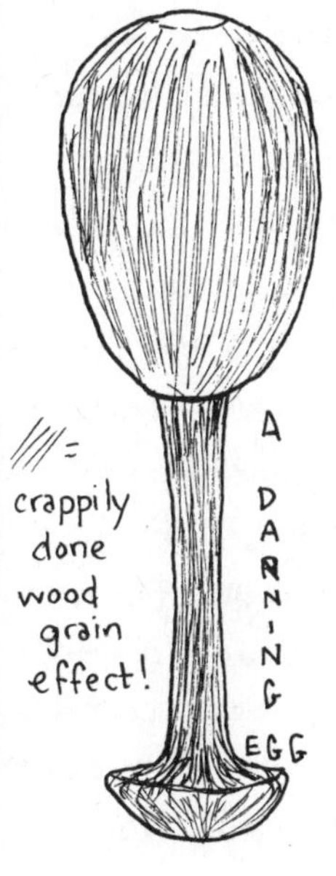

Darning is easiest if you acquire a thing called a darning egg. It looks like a chicken egg with a handle attached. The egg works by providing a surface for the fabric to lie on top of, so that the edges of the hole don't get distorted. If you don't have a darning egg, you can place your non-sewing hand underneath the fabric—just try not to stretch or bunch the fabric as you work.

Step 1: Place the darning egg (or your hand) underneath the hole.

Step 2: Using strong thread and a darning needle, create a running stitch that begins beneath and to one side of the hole and goes straight across. When you're a little beyond the opposite edge of the hole, turn around and start a new stitch in the opposite direction. Work back and forth until you have a little square of horizontal stitches that extends beyond the hole on all sides.

Step 3: Without tying off, shift directions, and begin to weave by creating a vertical line of stitches over and under the horizontal stitches. Work back and forth, moving left to right (or vice versa) until all your horizontal stitches have been covered by vertical stitches. Knot off your thread and snip. Voila!

Hemming

Ah, hemming! The ultimate wardrobe-stretching skill. A good hem turns a bunchy, ratty-cuffed pair of pants into shorts you can wear for another few years. It's an essential skill for thrift shoppers, swappers, hand-me-downers, and anyone else who hates shopping for clothes. Learn to hem and watch the textile world open to you like a giant, machine-washable oyster.

Equipment:

- seam ripper
- tailor's chalk
- straight pins
- yardstick
- buddy and/or dress dummy
- iron and ironing board
- scissors
- needles
- thread—hem thread and a contrasting color for basting

Step 1

Use a seam ripper to gently release the existing hem. Pull out all the little thread squigglies as best you can without damaging the fabric.

Step 2:

Put on the garment along with shoes you plan on wearing with it. Grab a friend and some tailor's chalk to mark where you want your hem to fall. If you're hemming a skirt or dress, use a yardstick to measure the distance between the hem and the floor—make sure it's even all the way around. Mark the hem using chalk or straight pins placed parallel to the bottom edge of the fabric.

NOTE: No friends around? Consider getting yourself a dress dummy.

Step 3: Now, undress again and check your hem marks to make sure they're even. Do both pant legs match up? Does the hemline on that skirt wobble a little?

If your marks are uneven, use a clean toothbrush (or your finger) to erase the mark, and redraw it. Pin the new hem in place, put the garment back on, and check the hem again. Readjust as needed.

CHALK

Step 4: Once you're happy with the hem length, remove the pins and trim the bottom of the skirt/pant legs to their new length plus an extra 1½-2 inches for your hem allowance.

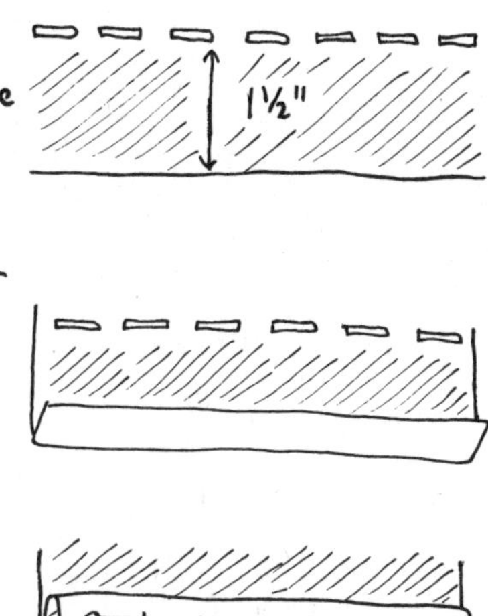

Then, create your new hem! Fold the bottom edge of your fabric up ½ inch, tucking the fabric inside. Press this lightly, then fold the fabric again up to the new hemline. Press again. Your chalk line should be on the very bottom edge of your garment. Pin the hem in place and baste to tack it down.

Step 5: Choose your stitch! If you're hemming casual clothes like jeans or a sundress, topstitch your hem using very small, even stitches. Make sure to choose a different color of thread than your basting thread. Once you're done, tie off

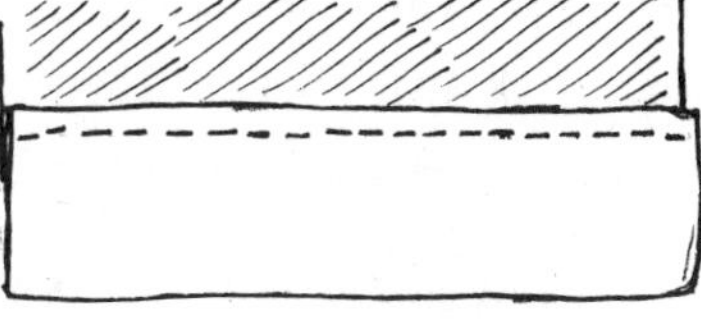

VS.

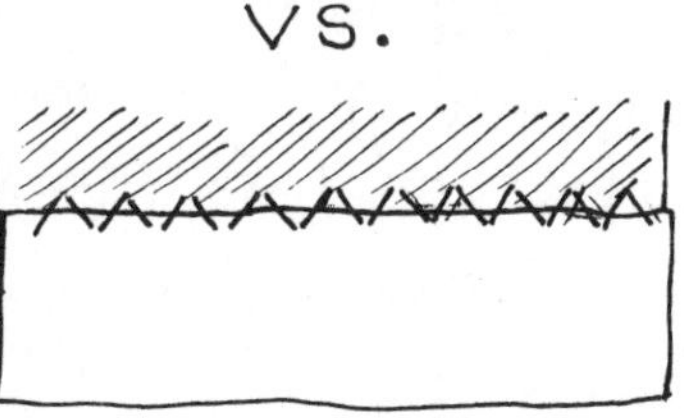

your thread on the wrong side of the fabric and remove your basting stitches.

If you're hemming dress pants or a garment on which a topstitched hem would look goofy, you should opt for an invisible hem. Baste first, then use a slipstitch to sew your new hem. See page 16 for instructions on how to create the discreet and lovely slipstitch.

Tips and Tricks!

★ If your hem looks a little fat, you can blame that first fold you made in your fabric. We do this because the fabric's raw edge can unravel if it's left hanging out. If you finish your edge with a quick overhand stitch, you can skip that first fold and thin out your hem.

★ Hems in knit fabrics like jersey are especially prone to coming undone. Hedge your bets by sewing twin hems, parallel to each other and about 1/4 inch apart.

★ Puckered hems can usually be pressed or steamed out.

Fixing a Zipper

Thousands of years of clothing technology and the zipper is still around? Ah, well. Here's how to resolve a few of the most common zipper mishaps.

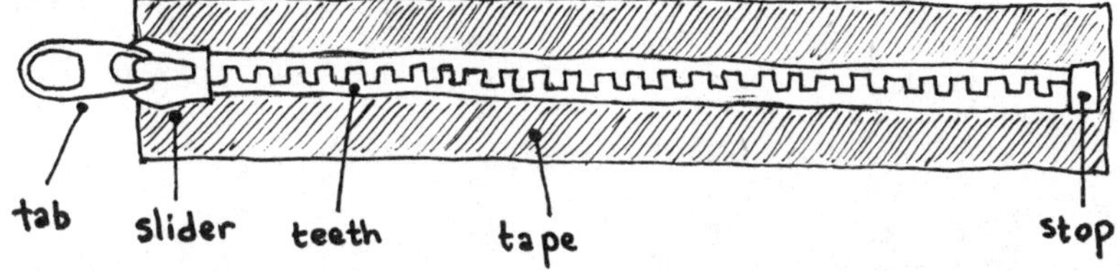

Sticky Zippers

First, if there is anything actually sticky on your pants, please wash it off. If your zipper still isn't working smoothly, you'll need to employ a non-messy lubricant to get the slider moving again. Your best bets are a bar of soap or the lead of a graphite pencil. Rub the soap or pencil up and down both sets of teeth, then zip and unzip a few times to get the stuff equally distributed. Wipe off any extra soap or graphite with a clean cloth. You may have to re-lube every few washes.

Slippy Zippers

If your zipper won't stay up, hold it in place with a finger and then shoot the teeth with a quick burst of hairspray. Yep. Try just a tiny bit at first to see if that fixes the problem, then add more if you need it. If you do this to a garment while you're wearing it (I have done this many times) you may want to shield the rest of your outfit with a towel.

Stuck Zippers

This one's pretty easy. There's probably a thread or a bit of fabric caught in your zipper. Grab some tweezers and fish it out. *Don't* try and force the slider past it. Be patient! Tug the slider around gently until you can see the obstruction and remove it.

No Tab (or Broken Tab)

You can fix a broken tab by squeezing the loop closed with some needle-nose pliers, but honestly? My favorite solution is to just replace the tab with a little bit of ribbon, canvas, or leather.

Slider Comes Off Part-Way

Step 1: Use a seam ripper and carefully undo the stitches that tack the zipper tape to your garment. Use needle-nose pliers to remove the metal stop from the bottom of the zipper. Slide the slider off of the zipper.

Step 2: Carefully realign the teeth one by one, and feed the teeth back into the slider. Go slow to make sure that the teeth are locking together properly. Zip the zipper up all the way.

Step 3: Use a needle and strong thread to make 10 or so tight stitches where the metal stop used to be. This will function as your new stop. Knot your thread well and snip it close so it doesn't get tangled in the zipper.

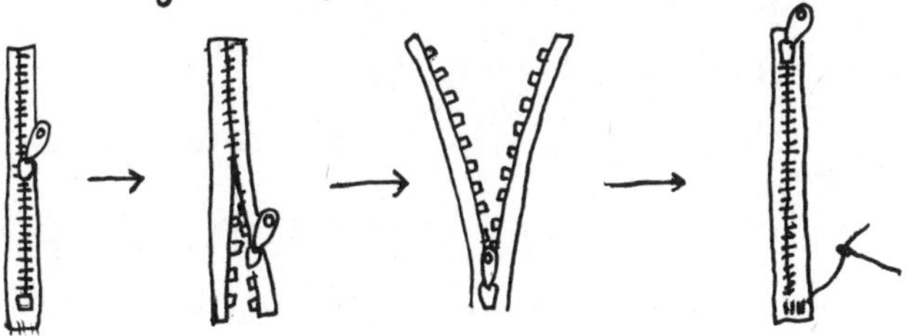

Gaps Below the Slider

This one is the worst! Sometimes you can hold one set of teeth firmly and nudge the other side up gently until they realign. But when things really go awry, you need to disassemble the bottom of the zipper.

Step 1: Grab your needle-nose pliers and remove the metal stop at the bottom of the zipper.

Step 2: Move the slider carefully down the zipper until it's right below the last pair of teeth. Don't remove the slider from the zipper, though!

Step 3: Smooth out the sides of the zipper and line up the teeth one by one. Feed the teeth slowly through the slider until you can see that they're locking up below.

Step 4: Create a new stop using strong thread, like you did in Step 3 on the previous page (the Slider Comes Off Part-Way section).

Waterproofing Canvas

Canvas is a beautiful thing, but when it mingles with rain, it can quickly become a mildew-speckled, sour-smelling disgrace. Removing mildew is probably not going to happen (ADMIT IT) so it's smart to avoid the nasty stuff altogether. It's pretty easy to make your own waterproofing formulas that you can use on tents, rucksacks, and any other piece of canvas that gets routinely exposed to the elements.

*Before you head off with that jug o' shellac, some caveats:

1. Waterproof canvas will keep rain off your back, but it will keep *in* all your sweat and body heat. So think long and heartily before you waterproof clothing.
2. Natural ≠ friendly. Unlike the recipes from Make Your Place, some of these formulas aren't exactly nontoxic. Do your waterproofing outside, wear gloves and old clothes, and keep kids and animals from getting into what you're making.
3. Don't inhale, eat, mainline, or otherwise absorb your waterproofing formulas.

WATERPROOFING SPRAY

*makes enough for one smallish tent

Mix together 2 cups soybean oil and 1 cup turpentine in a small bucket. Once the two liquids are blended, pour it in a spray bottle (use a funnel) and spray it onto your fabric. Or, keep the stuff in the bucket, and paint it onto the canvas with a brush or sponge. Use half the batch on one coat, let the canvas dry, and then do a second coat. Pay special attention to the seams and corners.

WATERPROOFING SOAK FOR TENTS

This option is messier than the spray, but if you'd rather dip your tent, here you go:

Step 1: Dissolve a pound of laundry soap (use a store-bought one with detergents in it) in two gallons of hot water. Stir well, until the soap bits are totally dissolved. Dunk your whole tent in the liquid, wring out the excess, and then dry it on a line or on the ground in a sunny spot.

Step 2: Dissolve a half pound of alum (check the hardware store) in two more gallons of hot water. Dunk the tent again and this time let it sit for a few hours. Wring it and let it air dry.

For maximum waterproofage, you should repeat this process every couple of months (if you use your tent often) or whenever you feel like it's getting leaky.

WATERPROOFIN' LEATHER

Lanolin is an oily substance derived from sheep's wool. It's an excellent waterproofer and pretty eco-friendly, too. (Just do a little research when you're shopping to make sure your lanolin is humanely obtained.) To use it, rub a bit into the leather with a soft cloth. Keep buffing until the leather feels dry (not greasy) to the touch. This also keeps the leather supple, which is nice.

If you have leather stuff but desire non-animal-derived waterproofing for it, petroleum jelly is a decent option. It's not earth-friendly, of course, but it's effective and cheap.

NOTE: Don't use either of these on suede—the oils will ruin the suede's nap. Honestly, suede is such a pain in the ass. Don't wear suede.

WATERPROOFING LIGHT NATURAL FABRICS

linen, hemp, and light canvas

NOTE: This may change the texture or appearance of your fabric.

Step 1: Gather a disposable paintbrush, some paper towels, a clean rag, and some beeswax.

Step 2: Melt the wax (stove or microwave) and paint it onto your fabric. Use paper towels to mop up leftover wax in the pan while it's still warm.

Step 3: Let the wax set overnight—I suggest laying it on a layer of old paper bags—and in the morning, buff the fabric with the rag.

WATERPROOFING NYLON

To waterproof nylon, you can use beeswax and the same method as for light natural fabrics. It might help to stuff the legs or arms with plastic while you're applying the wax, so that the hardening wax won't "glue" the layers of fabric together.

You also have your choice of vegan alternatives! Linseed oil or jojoba oil can be applied to a clean rag and then buffed into the nylon. Let the fabric sit overnight (or until it feels dry), and apply more coats if you so desire.

NOTE: You can get linseed oil from the hardware store and jojoba oil from the body care section of the health food store. If you decide to use linseed oil, make sure it's 100% pure linseed oil without any chemicals added. Also, linseed oil makes fabric stiff and sort of unattractive, so it's probably better for a backpack, bike cover, or tarp.

☆ waterproof ☆ jogging pants!

Sewing + Mending Resources

Martha Stewart's Encyclopedia of Sewing and Fabric Crafts (really, it's great)
by Martha Stewart
New York: Potter Craft, 2010

Stitch 'n' Fix: Essential Mending Know-How for Bachelors and Babes
by Joan Gordon
Lewes: Guild of Master Craftsman, 2009

Very Basic Book of Sewing, Altering, and Mending: 999 Pictures Show You How
by Violet Kathleen Simons
New York: Sterling Pub. Co., 1976

www.learningalterations.com

chapter 5

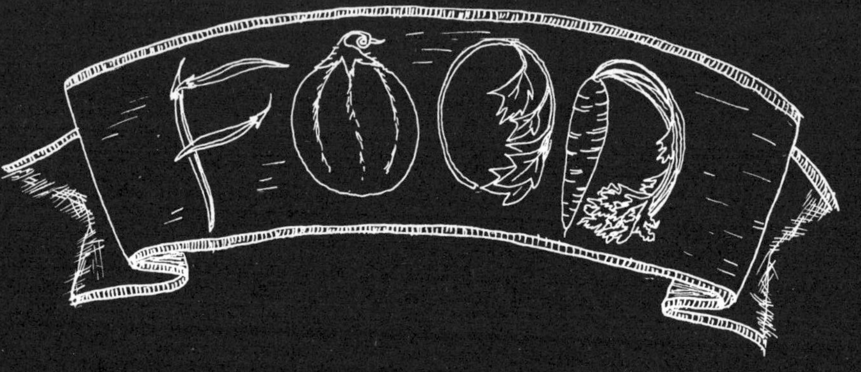

You know what's awesome? Growing food. And eating food. What's not quite as awesome? Figuring out what to do with the 50 lbs of zucchini getting flabby in your fridge. Never fear! This chapter is all about what to do with those delicious windfalls.

A lot of these processes will be familiar to many of you. Canning in particular is having a resurgence, and for good reason. It's really fun, delicious, and makes for great socializing if your friends are willing to help. That's the gift of DIY: it gives you a shared experience that lasts a lot longer than the quick buzz of a trip to the supermarket.

NOTE: Please play it safe whenever you're preserving food. That means using fresh ingredients, keeping everything clean, sterilizing equipment when you need to, and paying extra attention to food temperatures. Some of the processes in this chapter can take a long time, but cutting the steps short can lead to food that's unsafe to eat. Use your best judgement!

♡ Take care of yourself and each other. ♡

Storing Veggies

If you've ever tended a garden, you know that some years you might harvest nothing but three seedy, shrimpy cucumbers; other years, you might end up with more warty heirloom squashes than you know what to do with. It's the blessing and curse of every home garden. It's okay, though—if you're having a bountiful year and all your neighbors are *sick of your damn zucchini*, there are still plenty of ways to keep your harvest fresh until you eat it.

Preplanning Tips

Be realistic about what you can eat. It's fun to try new things in your garden, but if you're sowing a high-yield crop, take a moment to consider whether you'd be willing to eat it a couple times a week. Doesn't sound so appealing? Consider bartering or donating your excess veggies.

Make your own veggie dungeon. For a few of these methods, it helps to have a root cellar or something of that ilk, but any dark, well-ventilated space will work. Your veggies need to be kept away from heat and light, and many of them need a little humidity to keep them from withering. If you have a dark cabinet or other space, install a thermometer inside so you can monitor the temperature, and make sure there aren't any heating vents or heat sources nearby. If you're planning to store plants that like a little humidity (like carrots and turnips), you might want to add a humidifier or a few slightly damp towels that you can regularly replace and check for mildew.

Clean out your freezer or root cellar before you harvest. Any storage prep or preservation should happen as soon as possible after the plant is picked to preserve the fresh flavor and helpful enzymes of the food.

Harvesting

Handle with care. Fresh fruits and veggies are delicate, and unblemished specimens will store much better than bruised ones. Use a light touch to pick and clean your harvest, and throw out anything that's moldy or buggy.

Give underground-dwellers a little light. When onions, garlic, potatoes, and other below-ground edibles are dug up, their skins are still moist. Storing these freshly dug can lead to rot and mold. Instead, dig up these foods on a dry, sunny day and let them sit on the surface of the garden for a few hours afterwards. This will help their skins harden a bit, which will help them stay mold-free for longer.

Storing Produce

Crate apples, pears, + roots

Most hardy fruits can be stored in wooden boxes on the shelf of your root cellar or storage area. The key here is to keep the pieces from touching each other, to protect the fruit from rot or fungus. One way to accomplish this is to wrap each piece in waxed paper, parchment, or even newspaper. Pack them in a single layer, pad with crumpled paper, and repeat. If you're more ambitious, you can swap the paper for barely moist sand or dry sawdust.

The sand/sawdust route also works for carrots, beets, and other roots. Brush any excess dirt off the roots first (don't wash them), and lop off the greens to keep them from pulling nutrients from the root. Make a thin layer of sand on the bottom of the crate, then lay down a layer of roots, making sure the roots don't touch each other. Add sand around and onto the roots, and repeat.

Hang pumpkins, squash, onions, and garlic

Easy and fun! You can get really creative with your hanging techniques (garlic garlands!), but storing these long-storing veggies can be as simple as dropping the bulbs or squashes into an old pair of stockings, tying a knot between each bulb to keep them from touching, and then hanging the whole shebang up in your root cellar. If it doesn't look nice enough, use prettier stockings. :)

Bag potatoes

Potatoes keep well in a plain old paper bag, as long as the humidity is kept as low as possible AND they're kept away from light. If you live in a humid climate, you can cure your potatoes first by letting their skins toughen in the sun for a few hours before you store them. Don't wash before you bag—just brush off the excess dirt with your hand or with a dry brush. If you're worried about sprouting, toss an apple in the bag with the potatoes. It works, somehow.

Dry beans, fruits, mushrooms, peppers, and tomatoes

Drying a food obviously alters its appearance and texture, so it's not ideal for every purpose, but dried food does last a really long time. It saves space and weight in your pantry, kitchen, backpack, or whatever.

I'm not going to include instructions for dehydrators here, because I don't own one. I'm sure it's a lovely tool to have, but it's not absolutely necessary. All you really need is an oven, some counter space, and a day or two to let the process happen.

Maybe you're thinking: "doy, Raleigh, why can't I just leave my fruit in the sun?" Well, you can. It just takes longer, and you need reliably dry, sunny weather the whole time. So if you know you're gonna have a week without a cloud in the sky, go for it. Otherwise, use your oven like so:

Bean pods should stay on the plant until they're yellow and brittle. Then, cut down the whole plant and hang it up until it's completely dry. Sort through all the dry foliage, pull the beans out of their pods and let them dry indoors on baking sheets for a few more days. From there, you can pour them into airtight containers and keep around until burrito day.

Fruits (including tomatoes) are best dried in a warm oven (between 110 and 130° F). Slice apples and pears thinly. Berries and seedless grapes can be halved (if large). Tomatoes and stone fruits should be halved (and pitted, if applicable). Whatever you've got, spread it out on a baking sheet, sprinkle with sugar (optional—use salt for tomatoes) and dry in that warm oven for a day or so.

The fruit is ready to store when it looks and feels dry. You shouldn't be able to squeeze any juice out of it. Once it's fully dehydrated, keep the fruit in airtight jars. Eat it as-is, bake with it, or reconstitute it in a little boiling water.

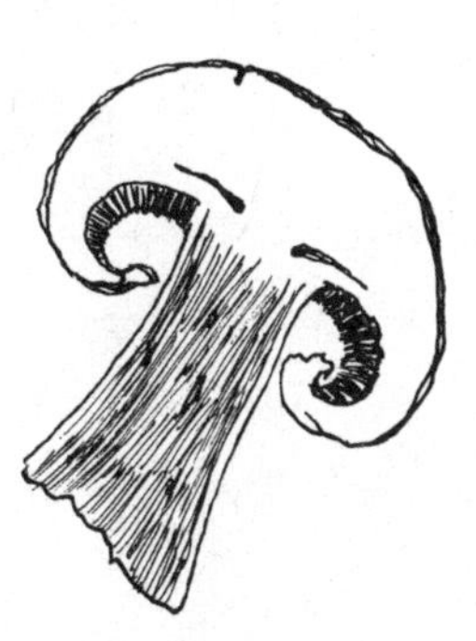

Mushrooms can be dried the same way as fruit (skip the sugar). Slice the bigger mushrooms and keep the little ones whole. You can also use a needle and cotton thread to string sturdier mushrooms onto a garland and hang them up to dry. Cute!

Peppers can be dried like fruit in a 140° oven, OR you can string them up in bunches and let them dry in a warm, ventilated area.

Freeze peas, beans, corn, and other delicates

Spring and summer's eager, plentiful veggies don't store well, so freezing is a good option. As soon as possible after your harvest, create a little assembly line like so: Have a big pot of water boiling on the stove; a bowl of ice water close by; a colander by the sink; and a baking sheet on the counter.

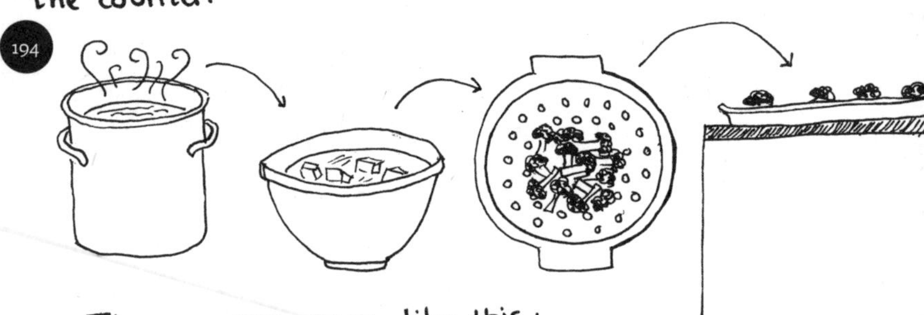

The process goes like this:

<u>Step 1</u>: Clean and prep a small batch of veggies.

<u>Step 2</u>: Blanch the veggies in water for 1-2 minutes. For bigger chunks like broccoli florets, blanch a little longer. Corn on the cob should boil for at least 5 minutes.

Step 3: Using a spider, tongs, or a slotted spoon, remove the veggies from the boiling water and dunk them into the ice water.

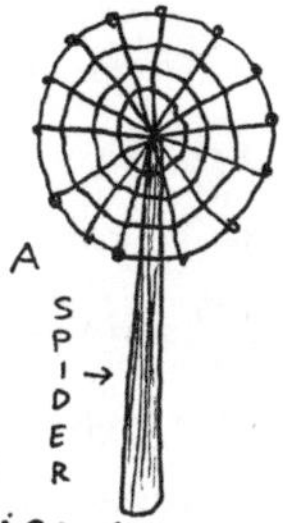

Step 4: While the first batch is cooling, prep the second batch and add those veggies to the boiling pot. Start your timer!

Step 5: Remove the veggies from the ice bath and let them drain in the colander.

Step 6: Continue like this until all the veggies have been blanched and cooled. Dry the veggies in the colander with a towel and then spread them on the baking sheet in a single layer.

Step 7: Pop the baking sheet in the freezer. This will allow each chunk of vegetable matter to freeze separately, eliminating any clumpy masses of frozen crap later. Once frozen, pop everything in plastic bags and label them.

Clamp a ton of root vegetables

Do you have mild winters and a veritable buttload of root vegetables? Congrats! Clamping might be your jam. A clamp is very literally a food pyramid, created outside and covered with earth and straw. This is a little impractical for most people, but if you have a large garden (or a small farm), it's a great, traditional way to store tons of food without encroaching on anyone's living space.

To make a clamp, you'll need a bare patch of ground and loose, dry-ish soil, plus a shovel and some dry straw. Harvest your roots and let them sit on top of the ground while you site and start building your clamp.

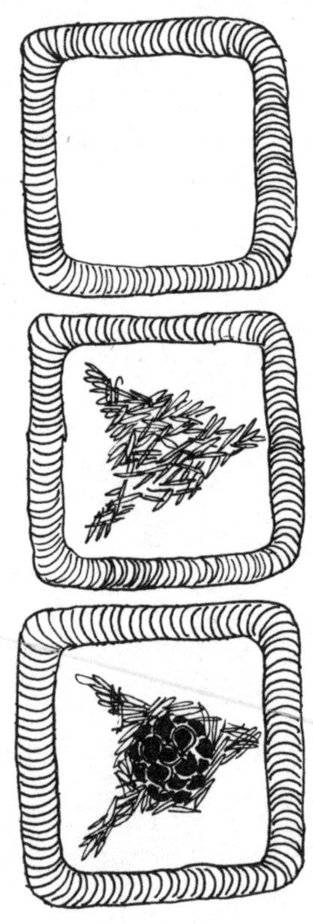

Step 1: Pick a spot that tends to stay dry (under an eave is good), and dig a trench around the area to keep the clamp site from getting soggy.

Step 2: Make a nice layer of straw for your veggies to rest on. Add a couple of "legs" to the straw layer by building little tunnels outward from the main pile.

Step 3: Pile the roots on top in a mound shape and cover with more straw. Let the clamp sit for 24-48 hours to allow any moisture from the roots to evaporate.

Step 4: Using a small shovel or spade, pile earth on top of the clamp. Leave the legs uncovered — they'll act as vents to keep air circulating around the roots. Build the clamp in a pyramid shape until you've added about 5 inches of dirt on every side.

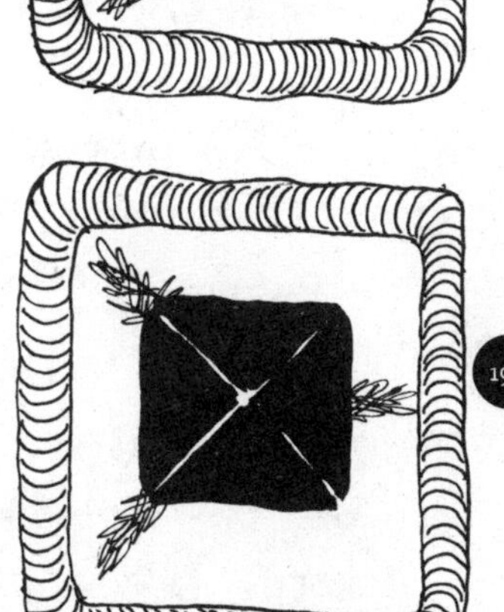

Step 5: Pack the top layer down nicely and keep the walls steep so that any rain that hits it will roll right off.

AND NOW YOU HAVE A CLAMP!

Crap! My carrots have gone limp. ӛ

★ To revive flabby vegetables like carrots, celery, potatoes, or lettuce, wash what you've got and then soak those suckers in ice water + 1 T vinegar for up to an hour. Should be firm and sprightly by then.

drying herbs

Drying herbs is a simple, effective way to preserve most of their taste, color, and medicinal properties. Dried herbs might not taste exactly like fresh ones, but in the middle of winter a little bit of summery flavor goes a long way.

As for process, you've got a veritable glut of options. But you'll want to start by:

Prepping Herbs for Drying

* Harvest herbs when your plants are preparing to blossom. The plant's leaves will be full of essential oils, which is what you want.

* The best time to gather herbs is in the morning after the day's dew has evaporated. Mid to late summer is perfect, because the days will be warm and dry and most leafy herbs will be at their peak.

* Herbs should be cleaned carefully to avoid scrubbing off any aromatic oils. A rinse in cold water will do the trick. Afterwards, gently shake the herbs and let them air dry completely. Pick off any dead or gross leaves and compost them.

* Once your herbs are dry, they should be stored in an airtight container away from light, heat, and humidity. You can crush them or keep them whole.

Bunch Drying → for herbs with lengthy stems

Step 1: Snip and wash your herbs.

Step 2: While the herbs are air-drying, grab a paper bag and open it up. Use a pokey instrument (knitting needle? BBQ skewer?) to punch several holes in each side of the bag.

Step 3: Bundle your herbs and tie the stems together with twine. Stick the tops of the herbs inside the bag and gather the top of the bag around the stems. Secure the top of the bag with more twine.

Step 4: Hang the whole contraption somewhere warm, well-ventilated, and away from direct sunlight. (The doorway of your kitchen might be perfect.) The bag is optional, honestly, but it will provide further sun protection and keep the herbs from getting dusty.

Flat Drying → for seeds + herbs with short stems

Step 1: Prep, wash, and dry your herbs.

Step 2: Lay the herbs in a single layer on a baking sheet (or two). Cover the herbs with a clean tea towel and place the tray in a warm area where it won't be disturbed.

Step 3: Stir the herbs every few days to make sure they're drying evenly.

Cool Oven

↳ for large quantities of herbs + for impatient people

Follow steps 1 + 2 of the flat drying method. The warm place you'll use will be your oven, heated to only ~ 180°F. Prop the oven door open a little and leave the herbs there for a few hours. Stir the herbs gently every hour to make sure they're not sticking, scorching, or drying unevenly.

Even Cooler Oven → for non-bakers

* NOTE: Needs a gas oven

Follow the directions for the cool oven method, but don't turn the oven on. Leave the herbs in there for a day or two and the pilot light will dry them out.

NOTE: This method obviously works best if you don't bake a lot. Make sure to take the herbs out of your oven before you use it or else: scorch city.

Microwave → for woody herbs

Step 1: Spread clean, ABSOLUTELY DRY herbs on a paper towel.

Step 2: Nuke the herbs on high for 1 minute. If the leaves are still supple, nuke for 30 seconds more.

Step 3: Repeat step 2 until the leaves are dry and brittle. Let them cool on the counter.

NOTE: You really have to do this 30 seconds at a time to prevent *fire* and *scorching*. BE PATIENT!

Freezing → for when drying won't cut it

Dry basil or cilantro will do in an absolute culinary emergency, but let's face it: they suck. So what's a gardener to do? Freeze those suckers fresh + preserve that flava. After you prep, chop the herbs + freeze them in a single layer on a baking sheet.

OR! Blend the herbs with a little water, broth, or oil and put one teaspoon in each section of an ice cube tray for pre-measured herbs at the ready!

Tangent: one of my first forays into DIY herbal work involved sticking a few sprigs of sage into an old bottle of vinegar from the kitchen. I didn't eat a lot of salad back then (I was a teenager), but I used it in my bathwater + on my zitty face and it was just fabulous. Herbal vinegars: so simple even a 15-year-old idiot can make them. Anyway.

Herbal vinegars capture the flavor of an herb in a tasty, shelf-stable liquid form. They're perfect for using in marinades, vinaigrettes, or on fresh fruit. Or, as my story suggests, you can use them for cosmetic or medicinal applications.

To make herbal vinegar, all you need to do is infuse a good quality vinegar with fresh herbs and let it steep in a dark place for about a month so all the flavors of your concoction can blend. Then, strain out the solids and let it sit for another week or two until the flavors are pleasingly mellow.

The proportion of herbs to vinegar is important, but it's not set in stone. Start with a few big sprigs of fresh herb per cup of vinegar, and let it steep for a couple of weeks. If it still tastes weak, you can add a bit more.

The type of vinegar you use depends on what you're using the finished product for. Apple cider vinegar is full of nutrients and is perfect for cosmetic and medicinal blends, but the taste is a little too strong for most people. White wine, red wine, sherry, and rice vinegars are great bases for culinary herbs.

Herbal Vinegar Ideas

- ★ white wine vinegar + chives, sage, thyme, or rosemary (+ lemon peel?)
- ★ red wine vinegar + basil or oregano, or really any Italian herb
- ★ sherry vinegar + tarragon or ramps
- ★ apple cider vinegar + fresh raspberries or strawberries

HOT TIP: Want something a little stronger? Swap the vinegar for decent vodka, brandy, whiskey, or rum. Steep for a month, strain, then make into cocktails that cost $10 each.

Herbal Syrups & Honeys

True fact: An herb-spiked simple syrup or honey will take your next batch of cocktails to the NEXT LEVEL. Also going to the next level: lemonade, iced tea, soda water, pound cake, and anything else that calls for a glaze or liquid sweetener.

Herbal syrups are super easy to make, and the recipe multiplies well, so you can whip up a batch whether you have bushels of herbs or just a few sprigs. So next time you find some extra-fragrant rosemary growing on the sidewalk, grab it—you won't regret it!

Basic Herbal Syrup

1 cup sweetener, like sugar or agave

1 cup water

A dozen or so herb sprigs, or a big hand-

-ful of fresh leaves.

Step 1: Stir water and sugar together in a small saucepan and bring to a boil on the stove. Stir until all the sugar is dissolved. If sugar crystals form on the sides of the pan, wet them down with a wet pastry brush.

Step 2: Add the herbs and crush them into the pan with your spoon. (Don't bruise them with your hands—you want the oils to release into the sugar mixture, not onto your hands.) Cover the pot, and let the herbs steep for up to an hour.

Step 3: Using a sieve and a funnel, strain your syrup into a jar or a bottle with a tight-fitting lid. Leave an inch or so of headspace in the jar, in case you decide to freeze the syrup later. Press the remaining herbs with your spoon to get the last drops of syrup out, then toss the herbs in the compost bin.

★ herbs to try ★

- ★ rosemary
- ★ thyme
- ★ rose petal
- ★ violet
- ★ lavender
- ★ lemon verbena

Step 4: Label your syrup! This will keep for up to a month in the fridge or a year in the freezer.

Herbal Honey

2 cups light-flavored honey, like clover

1 tablespoon of fresh herbs, ground well (or you could use 1 teaspoon dried)

Cheesecloth

Step 1: Wash and prep your herbs, then tie them up in the cheesecloth.

Step 2: Put the honey and herbs into a heavy-bottomed pot and warm it over low heat. If you're using raw honey, heat the honey only until it's warm.

Step 3: Pour the whole shebang into a mason jar, seal it up, and let it sit in a dark place for two weeks (longer for more intensely flavored honey).

Step 4: Heat the honey again; remove the herbs and squeeze out any honey. Strain the honey back into the jar.

Herbal Blend Ideas

★ For tea parties: lavender, rose petal, or fennel seed

★ For colds: lemon balm, rosemary, or mint

★ For bedtime: chamomile or lavender

Canning

Canning is arguably the most popular form of food preservation right now, and for good reason: homemade pickles, preserves, and jams are among the most delicious things you'll ever eat. I am completely biased. But if you grow great produce or know where to find it, there's nothing more rewarding than being able to save those perfect berries and incredible vegetables for a dark, dreary winter day.

Also, people freak out over homemade jam, and pickling parties are really fun. So there's that.

I'm only providing a couple basic recipes in this book, because there are hundreds of canning books out there right now. You might notice I'm only talking about jams, jellies, and pickles, and not including stuff like canned meat or non-pickled veggies. That's because those foods can't be canned safely without a pressure canner, which can heat food to a higher temperature than a

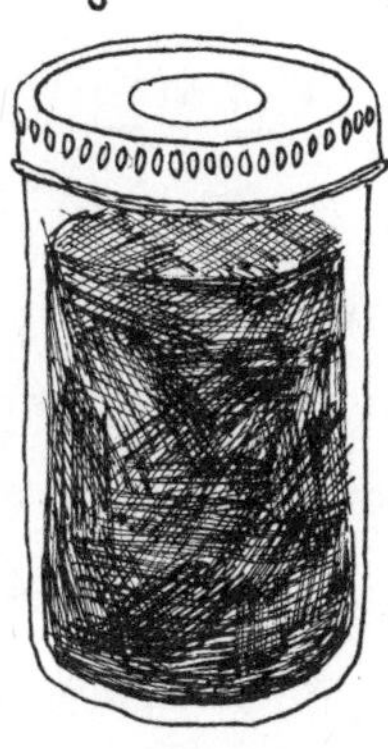

pot of boiling water can. This section is mainly for beginners, so pressure-canner recipes are a bit out of scope.

Supplies

You can find tons of tools that purport to make canning less labor-intensive, but the truth is that it's a long process no matter what. Unless you're starting a jam business, I suggest you start with the basics. And here they are!

A Cooking Pot: Use a big, heavy-bottomed pot (6–8 quarts) that's wide enough to cover your stove's largest burner. Material is important here: pickles, jams, and preserves all require some kind of acid, so a non-reactive pot is essential. Choose stainless steel or enamel and you're good to go.

A Boiling Pot: This mother needs to be BIG, at least 9 quarts, and bigger if you plan on canning large or multiple batches at once. Make sure it's deep, too, so that the jars can be completely covered without causing any boilover.

There needs to be some kind of rack in the bottom of the boiling pot to keep the jars from bumping around. You can buy a rack, or you can improvise by adding a metal trivet or folded dish-towel to the pot before you fill it up.

Jars, Rings, and Lids: Use Mason or Ball jars, *not* old pickle or mayo jars from the store. That will end in tragedy, or at least failure.

Canning jars are easy to find at grocery or thrift stores. Rings and jars in good condition are fine to reuse, but buy new flat lids each time you can. Once you crack the seal on a jar of home-canned food, the lid can't be reused. Sorry. :(

Other Tools, in no particular order:

* a jar lifter (sooo much nicer than tongs!)
* a wide-mouth funnel
* a sieve (if you're making jelly)
* a candy thermometer
* a kitchen scale
* a wooden spoon
* a chopstick
* a ladle
* a small, heatproof bowl

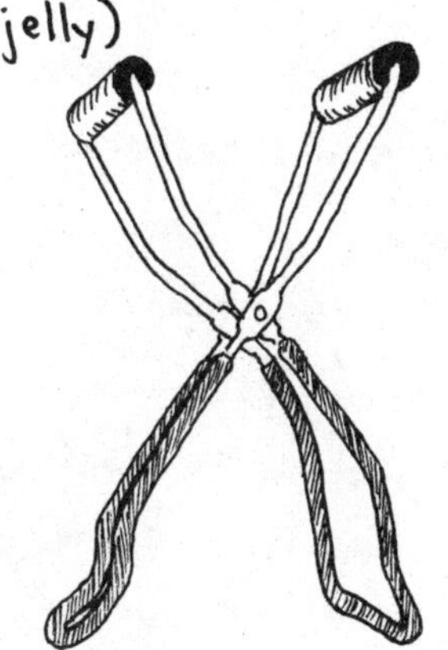

The Process goes like this:

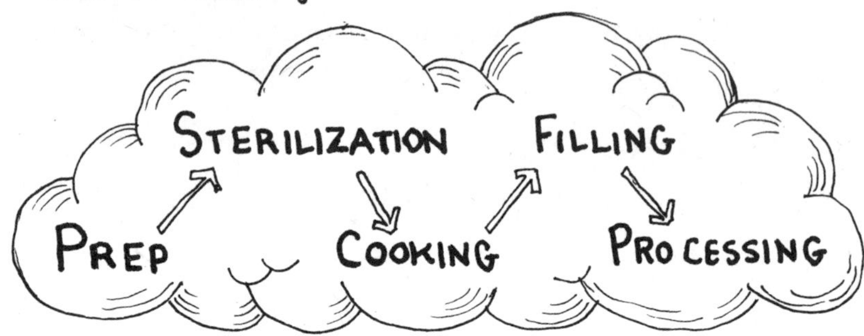

Step 1: Prep your fruit or veggies. If you're making jam, this might mean hulling strawberries or pitting apricots. For pickles, it might entail lots of chopping. Either way, get it done with and have your ingredients prepped and measured ahead of time.

Step 2: Start your hot water bath for later on. Fill the boiling pot with water, add the jar rack, and put it on the stove over high heat.

Step 3: Wash your jars, rings, and lids. Place the lids in a heatproof bowl, and have the rings next to them on the counter. Place the clean jars on a folded towel (we'll call it a prep towel) near the boiling pot. While you're at it, put another folded towel (the cooling towel) nearby to hold the jars after they come out of the water bath. Grab the jar lifter, funnel, ladle, and chopstick, and have them nearby, too.

Step 4: If your recipe calls for a processing time of 10 minutes or less, sterilize your jars before you fill them. Once the water boils, use a jar lifter to put the jars in one by one. Keep them submerged for at least 10 minutes.

Step 5: Make your preserves, pickles, or whatever delights you have in store.

Step 6: When the jars are sterilized, use the jar lifter to carefully lift the first jar out of the water bath. Pour the water from this jar into the heatproof bowl, on top of the jar lids. A warm bath will soften the rubber on these guys and help form a tight seal later on. Remove the remaining jars from the water bath, tip the water from each into the pot, and place them on the prep towel.

Step 7: Using the ladle and funnel, pour your brine or jam into the hot jars. Leave about 1/4" of headspace in each jar (this might vary by recipe).

Once the jars are full, run the chopstick around the inside of each jar to remove any large air bubbles. Wipe each jar's rim with a damp towel.

Step 8: Plop a warm jar lid on each jar. Add the ring and screw it on until it's just tight—don't force it! A lid that's too tight will trap any lingering air bubbles inside, which is bad news.

Use the jar lifter to place the jars upright in the water bath. The water should cover the jars by at least an inch or two. Boil away for the length of time designated in your recipe. Then, lift the jars out and place them on the cooling towel.

Step 9: Leave these babies alone for an hour or two, then do a pop test on each lid to make sure it sealed properly. If the lid pops up and down when you press it with a finger, your jar isn't sealed. Ain't no thing, though: you

can still stick the jar in the fridge and use what's in it. It's just not shelf-stable.

Once the jars have cooled completely, remove the rings and store the jars in a cool, dark place. Why remove the rings? To detect botulism, of course! Dangerous bacteria get very active in an environment like a poorly sealed jar. If your jar has nasties in it and the ring's off, the pressure inside will force the lid to pop off. Thus, you know not to eat whatever's in there. Better messy than sick, amiright?

★ ★ ★

★ Simple No-Pectin Jam

★ makes ~ 2 quarts

4 lbs clean (peeled, seeded) chopped fruit

4 c sugar

4 T lemon juice (little less if your fruit is tart)

Pour all your ingredients into the cooking pot. If the fruit isn't super juicy, add 1/4 - 1/2 c water. Cook this mess over medium-low heat for about 2 hours, or until the temperature on a candy thermometer reads 220°F. At this point, your fruit will look suspiciously like jam. To test it, put a dollop on a saucer and stick it in the fridge. After a few minutes of chilling, the jam should be soft but not runny. If it's runny, cook another 15 minutes or so.

Ladle the jam into hot, sterilized jars, leaving about 1/4" headspace. Close up the jars like we talked about and process them in a water bath for 5 minutes to seal the jars.

★ Green Bean or Asparagus Pickles ★

*makes ~2 quarts

2 lbs clean, trimmed asparagus or green beans

4 cloves peeled garlic	2½ c cider vinegar
1 bunch fresh dill	2½ c water
4 t kosher salt	½ - 1 t chile flakes

Blanch the veggies + pack them into jars. Add a garlic clove and a couple dill sprigs to each sterilized! jar.

Bring the rest of the ingredients to a boil over high heat. Using a ladle, pour the hot brine over the pickles, submerging them + leaving 1/4" headspace.

Close up the jars and process for 10 minutes in a water bath.

Lacto-Fermentation

This method of preservation isn't quite as popular as canning, but perhaps it should be. Rather than using heat to kill off bacteria, lacto-fermentation uses bacteria to preserve food. The result is tangy, pickle-esque veggies and fruits bursting with healthful microbes. So all you kombucha freaks, pay attention: this one's for you!

The keys to successful fermentation are salt, time, and compression. The process is anaerobic, so you don't even need air—in fact air will only spoil the fun. You'll also need some tools you might not already have. The ideal fermenting vessel is a stoneware crock with a lid that can fit tightly inside it. You can find one in a specialty store or online.

Other equipment you'll need: a large rock to weigh down the lid, a large bowl, a sharp knife, and a large cutting board.

The most popular dishes prepared this way include sauerkraut and kimchi, but you can lacto-ferment all sorts of fruits, veggies, and even beverages. Give it a try!

<u>Sauerkraut</u> *makes 3 quarts*

5 lbs cabbage

3 T kosher salt

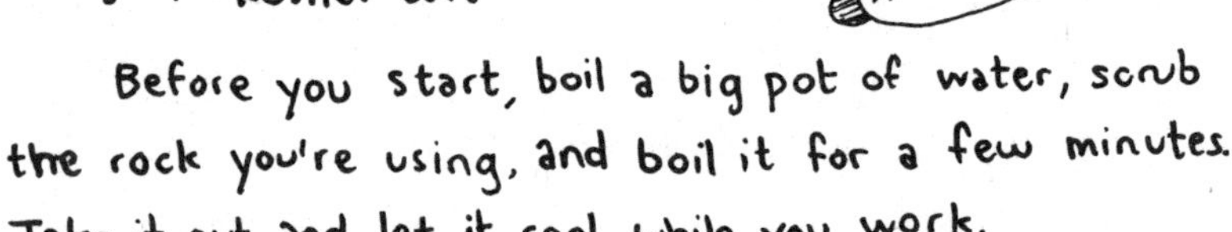

Before you start, boil a big pot of water, scrub the rock you're using, and boil it for a few minutes. Take it out and let it cool while you work.

Core the cabbage and slice it thinly. Place it in a large bowl and toss it with the salt.

Working a handful at a time, pack the cabbage into the crock. Really mash it in there! Once it's all in, smush the lid down on top of it and add the rock on top of that. Cover everything with a tea towel and move it out of the way.

Each day, push down on the rock to keep the cabbage tightly packed. Liquid will rise up around the lid, and that's great! It's just water drawn out by the salt. As long as the cabbage stays totally submerged in this brine, you're golden.

Let the cabbage ferment for two weeks. After about a week, try removing the lid and peek inside. You might see some bubbles or gross floaty spots. As long as these are on top of the liquid and not on the actual cabbage, there's no reason to freak. Skim off what you can and replace the lid and rock.

When two weeks are up, remove the kraut and put it into clean 1-quart jars. Keep these in the fridge and they'll last quite a while. Enjoy!

Lacto-Fermented Dill Pickles

makes 2 quarts

sour + salty—not vinegary!

10-12 pickling cukes, scrubbed and trimmed
2 T mustard seeds
1 T whole black peppercorns
4 big sprigs fresh dill
4 T sea salt
2 c spring water
2 grape leaves (optional—they preserve crispness)

Layer the ingredients in a fermenting crock. Make sure the water covers the pickles. Add the lid and rock on top (see Sauerkraut recipe). Let the pickles ferment for up to a week. Then, transfer them to the fridge packed in 1-quart jars. Again, you might notice a few bubbles here and there, but you're good as long as the pickles stay submerged. Your pickles will keep for up to 3 months in the fridge.

Making Jerky

I'm not going to ask why you have that much meat in your fridge. Maybe there was a sale. Maybe you and your friends bought a pasture-raised cow together + now your freezer's brimming with odd cuts you don't know what to do with. Maybe you found it! It doesn't matter. If you have lots of meat, make jerky. It's delicious, nutritious, and keeps long enough for you to actually finish it.

When choosing meat for jerky, pick a lean cut. The fat in meat is what turns rancid first, so fatty cuts of meat = nasty jerky. Big animals (cows, deer, elk) are popular for making jerky, but turkey and salmon work great, too.

Step 1: Using a sharp knife, trim as much fat as you can from your meat.

Step 2: Put a little bit of water or marinade in a pot and add the meat. Bring the liquid to a simmer and braise the meat until it's cooked through. Stick a meat thermometer in the pot to make sure beef, game, and fish reach 160°F;

Chicken, turkey, and other poultry should reach 180°F.

If you're wondering about why we cook meat before drying: while drying meat inactivates many harmful organisms, it doesn't kill them. They'll still be milling around in your meat until you cook it.

Anyway, once the meat is cooked, drain it and let it cool. Preheat your oven to 175°F.

Step 3: Place the meat on a clean cutting board. Use a sharp knife to cut the meat into thin strips (no thicker than 1/4"). Spread the meat on a baking sheet or two.

Step 4: Add seasoning! Salt at the very least, but I urge you to try out different spices, sugars, chiles, and citrus juices to see what tickles your fancy.

Step 5: Pop the meat in the oven, leaving the door slightly ajar, and cook the meat for about 5 hours. Successful jerky will be shriveled, dark, and firm but pliable enough to bend without snapping.

Step 6: Let the meat rest on paper towels to drain off any fat. When it's completely cool, keep the jerky in an airtight container for up to 2 months. Toss it out if it looks or smells moldy.

SALT-CURING FISH

These days, we tend to freeze food when we want to keep it on hand for a long time. Freezing is convenient, of course, but it's also a major trade-off. If you've ever defrosted a salmon filet to find it tasteless and dry, you know what I mean. A possible solution? Go super old-fashioned and try your hand at salt-curing.

Salt has been used to preserve food for basically ever. Packing meat and fish in salt (or alternately, soaking it in a brine solution) not only preserves the food, but infuses it with more flavor and a lovely firm texture.

Not gonna lie: this is a lengthy process. But if you like to fish or you participate in a CSA-style program, salt-curing will come in really handy when you suddenly have more fishes than one freezer can handle. You might say curing is really worth its salt! (But I won't.)

A few notes before you begin:

★ See if you can cure your fish in the summer, because you'll need plenty of sunshine and fresh air.

★ Salt curing, much like freezing, can affect the texture of your food. Salt draws moisture out of food, so salt-cured fish will be very firm and flaky. Plenty of people love this texture, but it may not be your thing. I say give it a try—if you don't like it, someone else surely well.

★ For salt-cure recipes, most folks use curing salt, which has large crystals that can soak up a lot of moisture. If you can find curing salt near you, awesome. If not, substitute any chunky or flaky salt, preferably one without additives like iodine. You'll need a lot of it (1lb salt for every 5 lbs fish), so choose something you can afford several large boxes of.

Coarse kosher salt is a terrific choice, as is Alaea salt or coarse sea salt.

Equipment:

★ fresh fish (sans heads, guts, and blood, and filleted off the bone)

★ lots of salt—see notes

★ a cooler or other large watertight container

★ a baking sheet or large, flat-bottomed bowl

★ a large, clean bucket for rinsing

★ clean wooden planks and non-metal weights
- for smaller jobs, you can use dishes instead of planks

★ a wooden clothes-drying rack or other wood frame

PHASE 1: THE SALTING

Step 1: If you need to, sort your fish by type—you'll need to preserve each type of fish separately.

Step 2: Coat the bottom of your cooler with a thin, even layer of salt. Grab a baking sheet or flat-bottomed bowl and pour a bunch of salt in that, too.

Step 3: Plop each piece of fish into the bowl or baking sheet and coat thoroughly with salt. Pat the fish down to make sure the salt's sticking.

Step 4: Place the fish inside the cooler in a single layer, skin side down. Top this off with a layer of salt, and repeat until all the fish are in the cooler. Flip the top layer so the skin side is up. Finish off with a final, even layer of salt.

★ don't overload your cooler! leave space

Step 5: Add a few wooden planks or dishes on top of the salt. Place the weights on top of the planks. As the salt draws moisture out of the fish, the salt will melt into a briny solution. You're adding the planks and weights to keep your precious fishes submerged as this brine starts to form.

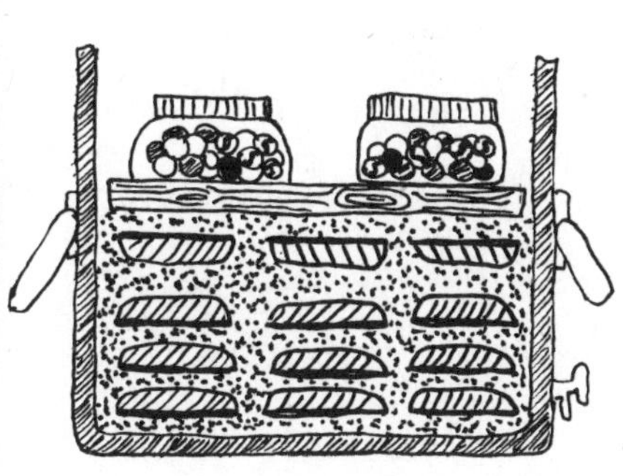

Step 6: Pop the lid on the cooler and let it sit for 2-3 weeks. The colder your climate is, the longer you'll have to wait.

Check your fish every couple days to make still they're still submerged in brine, and to add more salt to the solution. Don't forget this part! The fish can start rotting if the saturation level dips too much. Each time you add salt, put in enough so that no more will dissolve in the solution.

Do a smell test whenever you open up your cooler—you should smell fish, brine, and that's it. Grosser smells indicate something's gone wrong. The fish can be considered done (or phase 1 is, anyway) when the flesh is firm and translucent, and yields slightly when pressed. The fillets also might be a little smaller than when you put them in the cooler. If your fish stinks, is mushy, or is falling apart, toss it and scrub that cooler thoroughly with a baking soda paste.

PHASE 2: THE DRYING

Step 1: Prep a batch of fresh brine (make it about as salty as sea water) and pour it into a clean bucket. Dig the fish out of the vat and rinse them in the bucket to remove any excess salt.

Step 2: Transfer the clean fish to a flat surface and cover them with a new set of planks and weights. The pressing will squeeze out any remaining water in the fish and make air drying a lot quicker.

Step 3: Set up a wooden grate or frame (like a clothes-drying rack) in a dry spot outside. When the fish is no longer sopping wet, lay them over the frame in a single layer, flesh side up. Try to let as little of the fish touch

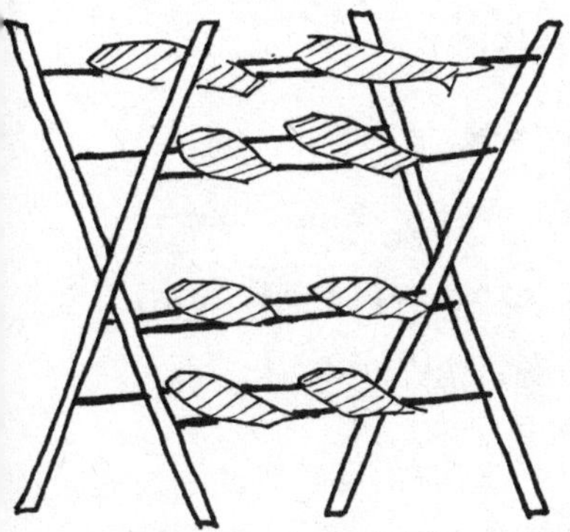

the wood as possible.

Let the fish stay here for a few days until each piece is thoroughly dry. Protect the fish from dampness as much as possible. That might mean moving the frame under an eave or into a ventilated shed during a rainstorm.

Fun fact: fish can get sunburn, even when they're dead. Too much sun can harden the fish's outer flesh and keep the inner flesh from drying properly. So if you can swing it, keep your whole apparatus partially shaded for the first day of drying, and then move it into direct sunlight for the rest of the drying process.

You can try this indoors if you need to, but keep in mind you need plenty of direct sunlight and serious ventilation.

When the fish is totally dry, pack it in an airtight container and either keep it in the fridge or a very cool, very dry place. If you have the means to vacuum seal the fish, so much the better.

Food Preservation Resources

<u>How to Store Your Garden Produce: The Key to Self-Sufficiency</u>
by Piers Warren
Totnes: Green Books, 2008

<u>Ball Complete Book of Home Preserving: 400 Delicious and Creative Recipes for Today</u>
edited by Judi Kingry and Lauren Devine
Toronto: Robert Rose, 2006

<u>The Canning, Freezing, Curing & Smoking of Meat, Fish & Game</u>
by Wilbur Eastman
Charlotte, VT: Garden Way Pub Co, 1975

<u>Wild Fermentation: The Flavor, Nutrition and Craft of Live-Culture Foods</u>
by Sandor Ellix Katz
White River Junction, VT: Chelsea Green Pub Co, 2003

chapter 6

For this final chapter, let's turn our attention to that very core of domestic life: our homes. Most of us face plenty of home-repair tasks on a regular basis—I rarely have days in which nothing in my home needs fixing.

There's a lot of apprehension about home repair because the stakes seem so high. But honestly, if you've ever cooked meat to a safe temperature or cleaned an oven without killing yourself, you can totally fix up your home. And you really should do the simple projects yourself, because DIY repair means less money spent on plumbers, less time spent waiting for your landlord, and less water and energy lost through drafty windows.

The how-tos that follow are for beginners or folks looking for a refresher. None of the projects involve blowtorches, caustic chemicals, or power tools, but I urge you to take proper precautions nonetheless. Make sure you have all your equipment before you begin, wear gloves and masks if there will be dust or chemicals around, and go slow until you have a good feel for the process. Have fun!

Ah, the paradox of doors: they pose some of the worst dilemmas, but also the simplest solutions. Don't wait until that handle breaks off and leaves you locked outside of your bathroom for hours! Doors are so technologically simple that minor annoyances like creaks, goofy handles, and loose hinges are easily overcome with the help of your tool kit. Here are a few of the most common door problems and how to fix them in a jiffy (or two).

Squeaky Doors

CREEEEEEEE...

So whenever you open this door, an ear-scraping squeak escapes from the hinges. How annoying! Conventional wisdom would have you grabbing the spray can of lube and blasting the hinges through that tiny red straw. Simple, right?

Not really. That stuff is great, but it can attract a lot of dust and gunk, thus rendering its lubricating qualities useless. Also, just spraying the whole hinge won't get to the root of the problem, which is usually the pin that's holding the hinge together.

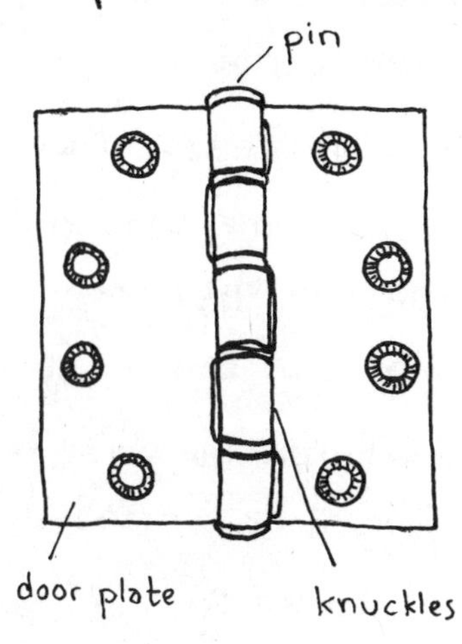

A better option is to remove the hinge pin and rub it down with white lithium, which is a thick greasy substance you can find at the hardware store. Once you're done, slide the pin back into place and tap it down gently with a hammer.

Sticky Doors

Another noisy problem: a door that rubs against its frame whenever you open or close it. This can happen if a door is cut poorly, set incorrectly in its frame, or if high humidity causes the wood to swell. To fix it, you first need to pinpoint which areas of the door are causing the friction.

Step 1: Grab a sheet of paper and a soft pencil and cover a good portion of the paper with scribbles.*

Step 2: Tape the paper over the top of the door in the spot that you think is rubbing. Open and shut the door a few times.

Step 3: Check your frame. Are there pencil marks on the door frame? If so, that's where your door is rubbing. Ding ding ding!

Step 4: Grab a sanding block, or a power sander if you have one, and sand down the troublesome area until the space between the door and the frame is clear. You might have to move the paper down and try sanding a different area if you couldn't pinpoint it the first time.

* You can also use carbon paper for this, but who has carbon paper?

Loose Doors

The swingin' nature of a door means that every door hinge will eventually get a little loose. Generally, this is caused by one of three things:

1. the screws are loosening due to the tug of the door being opened and closed;
2. the movement of the screws inside the door frame is causing the holes to become too big;
3. the screws were too short to begin with.

To figure out what's going on with your door, start by using a screwdriver to remove one screw from one of the door's hinges. Ponder this screw: is it only an inch or so long? If so, you probably just need a longer screw. Take the screw to the hardware store and find 8 new screws that look the same as the old one but are a bit longer. Replace all the screws on the frame side of both hinges.

Next, check out the hole where the screw used to be. Can you slide the screw into it without using your screwdriver? If so, you need to either fill in the hole a bit, or add a little something to your screw.

A good, quick trick to fix the first problem is to jam a couple of wooden toothpicks into the hole and break off any extra wood. Once the hole's full, replace the hinge plate and see if your screw doesn't bite a lot tighter.

If you need to amend your screw, try covering it with a layer or two of tinfoil. Tear off any excess foil once the screw's back in the door.

Removing a Broken Key

What a crummy situation! Well, hopefully there's more than one way into your home. The best way to remove a key from a lock is to spray the lock well with either liquid lubricant (like WD-40) or powdered graphite (which is slippery but not sticky), and then try to extract the key using needle-nose pliers. If you're using liquid lube here, make sure to wipe up any extra so that it doesn't attract dust.

Replacing a Doorknob

Don't put off replacing a shaky knob! It's way easier to install a new knob than to try and shove the handle back on after it falls off into your hand. All you need is a screwdriver and a bit of hand-eye coordination.

Before you get down to it, you need to find a new doorknob! Some things to consider:

★ Is this an exterior or interior door? If it's interior, do you want a lock on it?

★ Do you want a lever instead of a knob? If so, you'll need to look at your door and figure out whether you want your lever to be right or left-handed.

★ Try to find a replacement knob with a latch that's the same length as your current knob. If you can, remove the knob and latch before you go shopping and bring it in with you to compare. If that's not practical, you can pull the latch out, measure it, and screw it back in.

Step 1: Grab a bowl to hold any loose hardware. Open the door and pull up a chair. Have your legs straddling the door's edge so that you can easily access both sides of the door. Oh yeah, and grab a screwdriver.

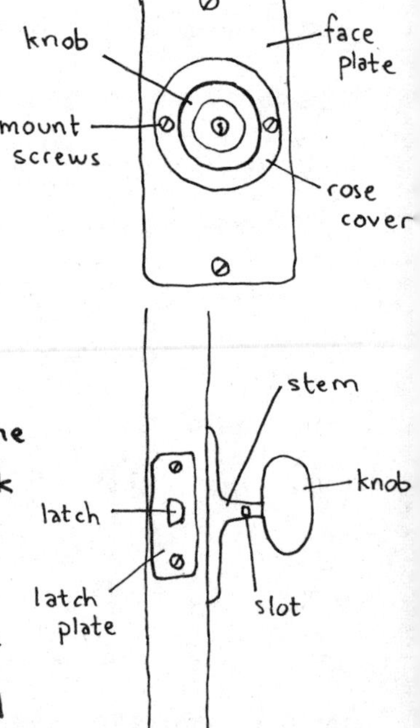

Step 2: Remove the screws on the faceplates. Remove the screws on the rose cover and pull off the doorknobs on both sides of the door.

NOTE: Some doorknobs have mount screws and some don't. If yours doesn't, look for a small slot on the knob's stem. Inserting a paper clip in the slot while pulling on the knob should release it from the door.

Step 3: With the knobs removed, you should be able to see the latch mechanism inside the door. Remove the latch plate screws and carefully slide the latch out of the door.

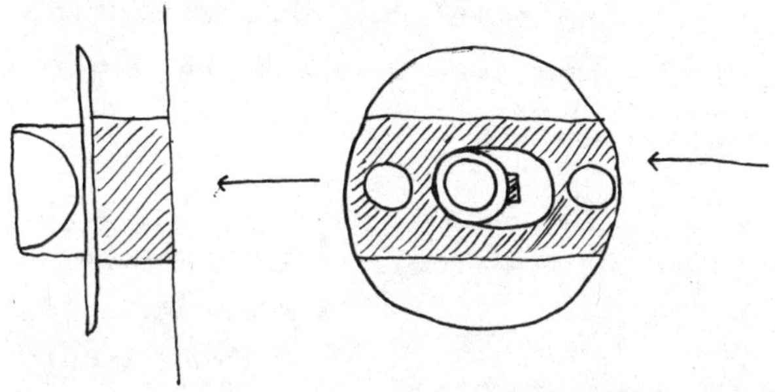

Step 4: Slide the new latch into the door and tighten the screws on the new latch plate.

Step 5: Align the stem of exterior knob so it slides easily into the latch casing. The stem will poke out through the inside of the door. Slip the interior knob over the stem.

Step 6: Replace the strike plate on the door frame. Make sure the lip of the plate faces the same direction it did before.

Step 7: Tighten the mount screws on the knob and plate and turn the knob to make sure the latch works.

PATCHING WALLS

And by walls, I mean drywall. Man, drywall just crumbles under pressure, doesn't it? It's a good idea to repair cracks and holes while they're still small. They'll definitely grow over time, and the bigger they are, the harder they are to fix.

What you'll need:

* Newspaper or drop cloth
* Utility knife
* drywall patch (for holes)
* drywall compound
* small brush
* paper dry wall tape (for cracks)
* wide putty knife
* compound tray
* sanding block and fine-grit sandpaper

Fixing Cracks

Step 1: Place the paper or cloth on the ground beneath the crack. Take a look at the crack and note its width. Will it be wide enough to fill with goop? If not, you'll have to widen it.

Step 2: Use the utility knife or the edge of your putty knife to remove rough edges and widen narrow parts of the crack. Sand it lightly if the edges still need work and use the brush to remove as much dust and grit as you can.

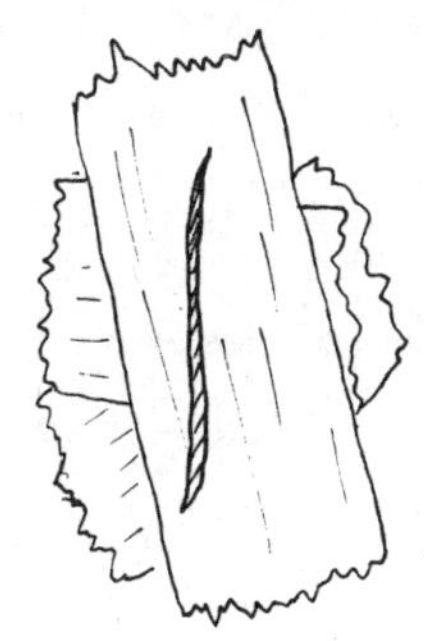

Step 3: Plop some compound in the tray and use the putty knife to coat the crack with compound. The compound layer should be thin and should extend a couple inches beyond each side of the crack.

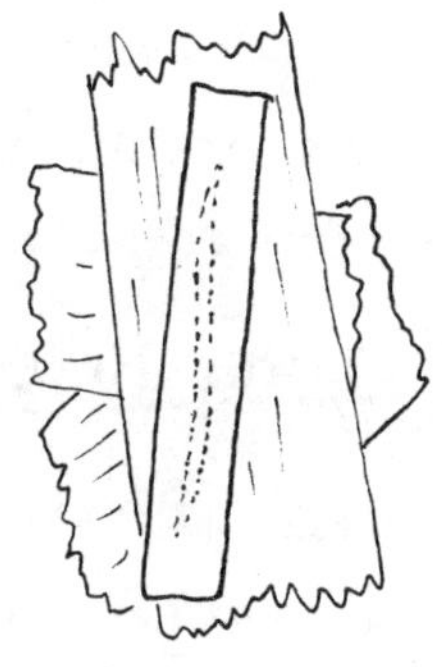

Step 4: Cut a length of drywall tape a little longer than the crack and stick it right on top of the wet compound. If the crack is crooked, you might need to use a few small pieces of tape instead. Make sure the tape is really embedded in the compound.

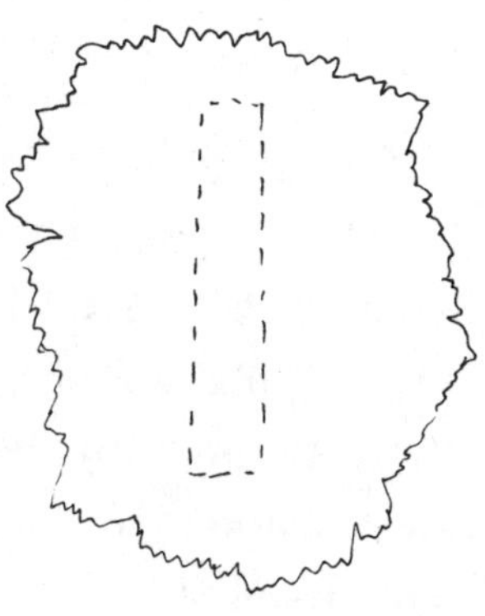

Step 5: Using a smooth scraping motion, swipe the putty knife over the top of the paper to remove any ridges. Load more compound onto the knife and apply another thin coat to the area. Feather the edges by moving the knife gently back

and forth as you work (this will help the repaired area blend into the wall once you're done). Let this dry overnight.

Step 6: The next day, apply a second thin coat of compound that's a teeny bit wider than the first. Let it dry and repeat with a third and final coat.

Step 7: Once everything is totally dry, use a sanding block and fine-grit paper to smooth the repaired area, especially the edges. Brush away any dust with a little brush. Finally, prime and paint the newly repaired area to match the wall around it.

Fixing Holes

Step 1: Place your drop cloth or newspaper under the hole. Use a utility knife to clean up the borders of the hole and remove any rough edges. Sand if you need to and brush off any dust.

Step 2: Cut the wall repair patch so that it's just big enough to cover the hole plus a little extra on each side. Place it over the hole, sticky side down, and smooth it with your hand.

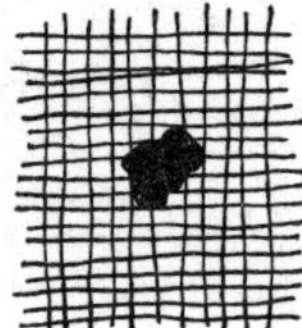

Step 3: Dump some compound into the tray. Apply a decent coat of compound on top and around the patch with a wide putty knife. Make sure the whole patch is covered. Vary your strokes and feather the edges of the compound coat. Allow the coat to dry.

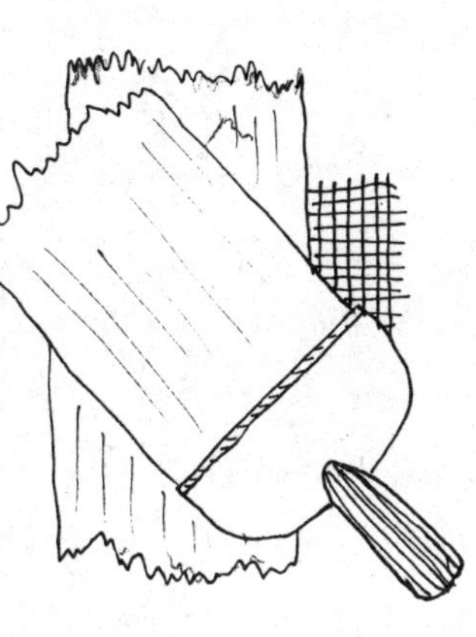

Step 4: Smooth out any bumps with your sanding block, then go over the patched area with another coat of compound. Dry again, sand again. Repeat! Once three coats of compound are dry and sanded nicely, feel free to prime and paint the wall to your heart's content.

Windows

Windows are more than just pretty holes in your house's face. They let in light, of course, but they're also responsible for regulating the (physical and, if you're into it, metaphysical) energy of your home. Anyone who's ever lived in an old house knows how much heat gets lost through drafty windows. Keeping windows operational and efficient can save you a ton of money, prevent wasteful energy use, and allow you to wear but one pair of socks in the wintertime. Hooray!

Opening a Stuck Window

There are a few reasons why a window might get stuck. Perhaps the humidity has caused the wood to swell and warp. Perhaps it's nailed or painted shut. Or perhaps it's just full of dirt and gunk. (Perhaps all three!) Such are the delights of living indoors.

Before you begin, check for nails or wedges that might be holding the window in place, and remove them. Next, check to see if the window's been painted shut. If so, here's what you can do.

Equipment:

* utility knife
* putty knife
* hammer
* candle stub
* toothbrush
* rag + cleaner
* sandpaper

Step 1: Use the utility knife to cut through the paint holding the window closed. Go slowly and don't force the knife.

Step 2: If that doesn't loosen the window, wedge the blade of a putty knife in between the window and its frame. You might be able to work the knife all the way around the frame, but if not, you can try tapping the end of the knife's handle with a hammer as if you were using a chisel. If the window isn't too far off the ground, you should try the putty knife trick from the outside, too.

Step 3: Open the window as much as you can, applying gentle pressure if necessary. Get a toothbrush or a small scrub brush and some cleaner and clean out the channels of the window as thoroughly as possible. Dry the channels with a rag, or let them air dry.

Step 4: Using sandpaper wrapped around your finger, sand the bottoms of the frame, the channels, and the bottom of the window. Look for any splinters that might be causing the window to snag and make sure they're sanded away.

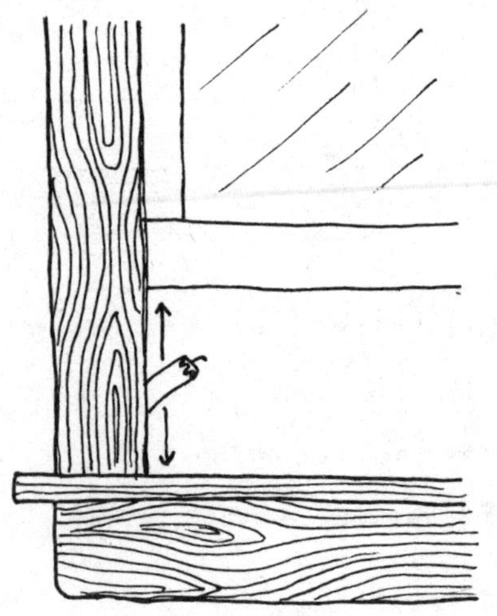

Step 5: Finally, run the stub of a candle up and down the channels of the window to lubricate them. (You can also use a chunk of beeswax for this.) Open and close window a few times to distribute the wax.

Repairing a Window Screen

My cat has a habit of climbing screens. Maybe yours does, too? In that case, it's helpful to know how to quickly patch a screen and get those claw-holes under control. (Your cat's behavioral issues are your problem, unfortunately.)

For tiny holes, use needle-nose pliers to bend the broken wires back toward each other. For bonus points, see if you can twist them together to strengthen the weak spot in the screen.

Larger holes in metal screens are patched with a bit of screen made of the same material. Make sure your patch is the same metal as the screen, or your screen may rust.

Step 1: Cut a square of screen that's a bit larger than the hole on all sides.

Step 2: Remove a couple of wires on each edge of the patch to create a fringe all around. Bend this fringe down at a 90° angle to the rest of the patch.

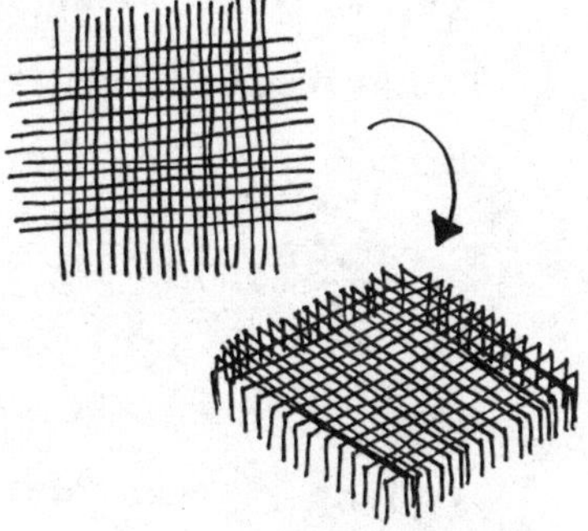

Make the angle as clean as you can.

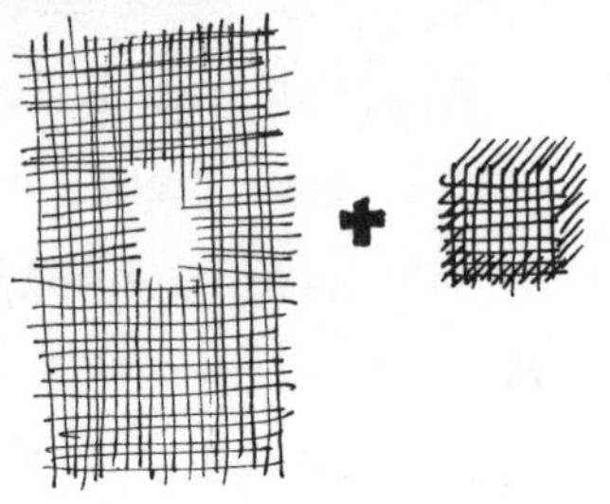

Step 3: Press the patch into the screen on top of the hole. Try to get the wires from the fringe to poke through to the other side of the screen.

If some of them splay out instead, remove the patch, realign it for a better fit, and try again.

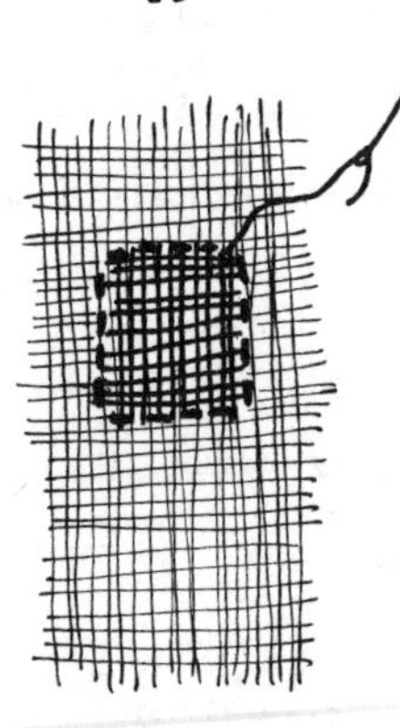

Step 4: Move to the other side of the screen and bend the fringe wires down so that they lay flat against the rest of the screen. If this feels weak, you can reinforce it by stitching the edges of the patch to the screen with fishing line or other strong thread.

NOTE: Plastic or fiberglass screens can be fixed by using a needle and fishing line to sew a piece of screen to the screen door, as if you were patching fabric. Waterproof glue will work in a pinch.

Fixing a Drafty Window

Old single-paned windows are generally pretty drafty—it's the price you pay for "old-world charm." But there's a lot you can do to increase the efficiency of your windows without paying out the butt for new ones. You'll actually end up saving money, because a drafty house costs more to heat. So there's that, too!

Before you can fix a draft, you need to find a draft. An old, reliable trick is to pass a lighted candle around the frame of the window. (Move any curtains out of the way first.) Go around the outside of the frame, too. If the candle flickers, air is leaking through in that spot. Mark the drafty spots with a sticker or pencil.

Depending on how quaky your candle flame gets, you might get away with a quick caulk touch-up. Or you might need to weatherstrip the window. Lucky for you, it's easy either way.

Equipment:

- silicone caulk
- rags and cleaner
- v-channel weatherstripping (vinyl is easiest)
- self-adhesive vinyl foam

Step 1: Clean and dry the sash, frame, and channels of the window. Most of the products used for weatherstripping depend on adhesion, and glue doesn't stick to dirt, unfortunately.

Step 2: Measure the window sash and cut two pieces of v-channel weatherstripping that are the length of the stile plus a couple of inches. With the window all the way open, remove the backing from one v-channel strip. Make sure the flared end of the v shape faces outside and press the strip into the window's channel. (If your strips aren't self-adhesive, use tiny nails or tacks to hold them in place.)

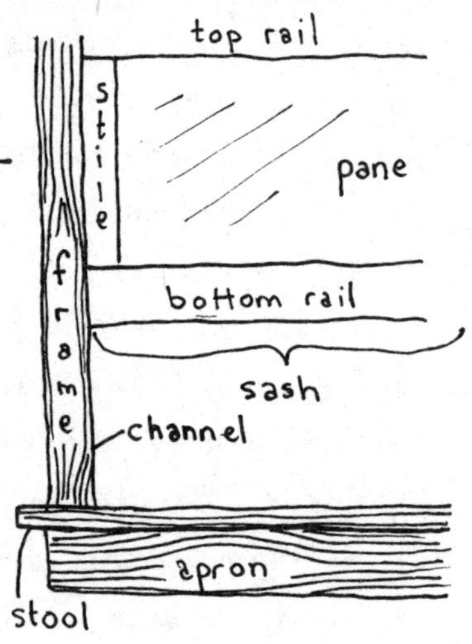

When you close the window, the strip should rise about 2 inches above the sash. Repeat on the other side of the window.

Step 3: Cut another strip of v-channel that will fit along the top rail of the sash. Open the window a few inches so you can stick the strip on the outside edge of the top rail. Face the flared end of the v shape upward, so that it gets squeezed shut when you close the window.

Step 4: Cut two strips of vinyl foam the length of the bottom of the sash. Remove the backing from the foam strips and press them into place along the bottom edges of the bottom rail.

Step 5: Seal the outside of the window frame with a thin bead of silicone caulk all the way around. Pay special attention to any trouble spots you identified earlier.

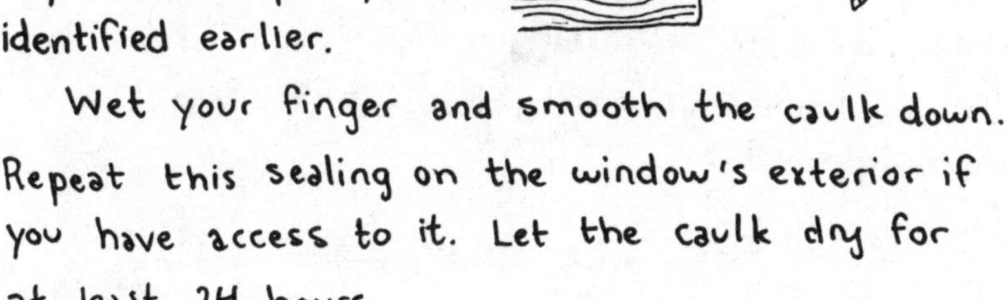

Wet your finger and smooth the caulk down. Repeat this sealing on the window's exterior if you have access to it. Let the caulk dry for at least 24 hours.

tubs and sinks

Want to drive yourself crazy? Think about drain openers for a second. They're effective, yeah, but they're also lethal. And they're meant for use in the parts of your home in which you spend your most vulnerable (naked!!!) moments. It gives me the heebie-jeebies. Lucky for us, there are plenty of ways to maintain your drains (and tubs, and sinks) without resorting to poison. Here are a few!

Unclogging Tubs + Sinks

For both sinks and tubs, your first course of action is to plug the overflow drain with a rag and go at the clog with your handy plunger. (Hint: a bit of petroleum jelly around the plunger's rim will create a tighter seal.) If that doesn't work, it's probably because whatever hair or gunk is caught in the pipe is too large to be dislodged by suction. Time for a bit of handsies-kneesies time. Don't forget your rubber gloves!

Equipment:

* rags
* screwdriver (flathead)
* clog-picker (a coat hanger, chopstick, whatever)
* a bucket
* needle-nose pliers
* adjustable pliers

Tubs

<u>Step 1</u>: If the tub has a stopper installed, remove it. Clean off any tangles of hair or gunk with a rag or paper towel, and set the stopper aside.

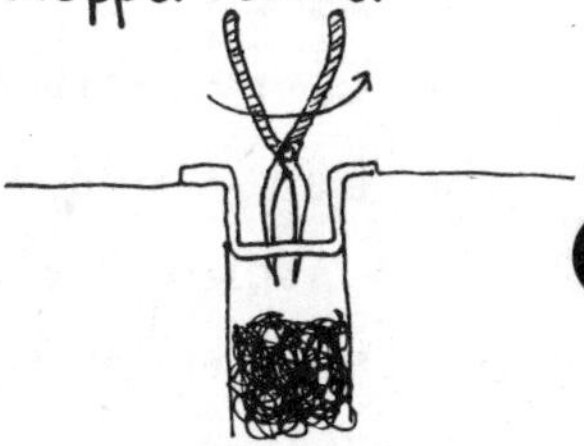

<u>Step 2</u>: Remove the drain cover by prying it up with a screwdriver or gripping the holes with needle-nose pliers and turning until it comes loose.

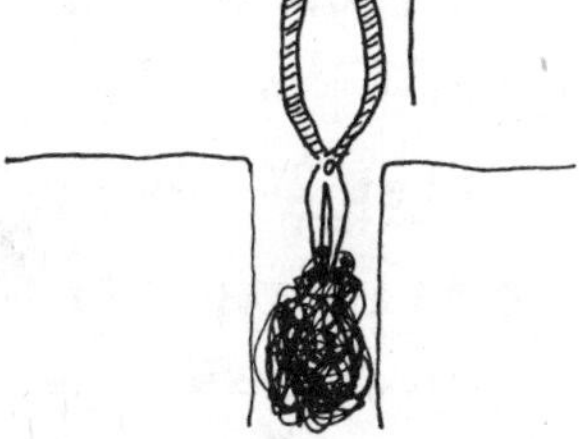

<u>Step 3</u>: Use a straightened coat hanger or your pliers, remove whatever's in the drain and throw it away. If the problem is just general gunk, try pouring a few kettles of boiling water down the drain to dissolve the buildup.

<u>Step 4</u>: Run some water down the drain to see if the drain's still clogged. If so, fill the tub a bit and

try the plunger again.

Step 5: Once the drain is clear, replace the drain cover and stopper.

Sinks

Sink clogs are usually the result of a clog in the U-shaped trap pipe under the drain. If plunging your sink doesn't do much, this pipe should be removed and cleaned out.

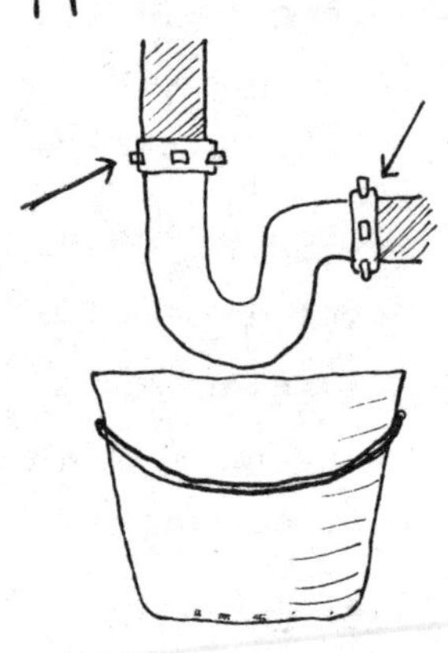

Step 1: Grab a bucket and put it directly beneath the trap. Using adjustable pliers, loosen the big slip nuts on the vertical and horizontal parts of the trap. Leave the nuts on the pipe as you remove the trap.

Step 2: Dump the water in the trap into the bucket. If your sink is really clogged, prepare for all the water from the bowl to gush down into the bucket as well.

Step 3: Use needle-nose pliers, a coat hanger, or whatever you have handy to remove the offending clog from the trap. If it's really gunky, you can use a rag or bottle brush to scrub the trap out (in a different sink, of course). If you don't encounter any clogs in the trap, check the drainpipe and the pipe in the wall—clogs like to hide there, too.

Step 4: Fit the trap pipe back in place and tighten the nuts with your fingers. Use the pliers to tighten them a little more, but not so much that it's hard to loosen them next time.

Recaulking a Tub

Bathtub caulk can get naaaaaasty, especially if (like me) you live in a mildew-prone climate. You can attack your tub with whatever cleaner you fancy, but eventually the mildew underneath the caulk will spread to the tile and the wall behind it. So replacing the sealant once in a while actually makes a lot of sense, as it can nip those big mildew issues in the bud.

When you're shopping, look for silicone caulk that's specially designed for bathroom fixtures. Get the kind you can squeeze by hand, because everyone knows caulk guns are a giant pain in the ass.

Equipment:

- silicone caulk
- masking tape
- caulk removal tool or razor blade
- rags
- vinegar, rubbing alcohol or bathroom cleaner

Step 1: Make sure the tub's dry before you begin. Apply masking tape directly above and

below the caulk all the way around the tub. This will help protect the tile from scratches as you remove the old caulk, and it'll give you a nice guide to work from while you apply the new stuff.

Step 2: Use a caulk removal tool or a razor blade to remove the old caulk. I recommend splurging on a caulk removal tool — at $7, it's easier to handle than a razor blade, so you're in less danger of hurting yourself.

Step 3: Once the caulk's gone, thoroughly clean the joint between tub and wall. White vinegar will do a good job, but some people prefer rubbing alcohol because it dries so quickly. And, of course, you can use your regular tub cleaner as well. Just make sure the joint is as clean as you can get it, and that it's totally dry before you apply new caulk.

Step 4: Fill the tub with water. The water weight will open up the joint between tub and wall, ensuring that your caulk will get into all the nooks it needs to.

Step 5: Open your new caulk and apply a thin bead of caulk to the joint all the way around. Use your finger (or the other end of the caulk removal tool, heeey) to smooth the caulk down in place. Carefully remove the tape, drain the tub, and let the caulk cure for at least a day before using the tub or shower.

Fixing a Leaky Faucet

There are a few varieties of faucet out there, and all of them work a little differently. Generally speaking, though, leaks are probably due to a worn-out washer, seal, or O-ring. To fix a leak, just dismantle the faucet until you find the faulty seal, replace it, and put the faucet together. Try a dry run (pun intended—turn the water off first!) before the repair to make sure you know the parts well.

Equipment:

- ★ rags
- ★ screwdrivers (both types)
- ★ Allen wrench
- ★ adjustable pliers
- ★ needle-nose pliers
- ★ spray lube
- ★ medium bowl
- ★ distilled vinegar
- ★ scouring pad

For all faucet repairs, your first steps should be to shut off the water to the faucet and plug up the sink with a stopper or rag. Pour some vinegar into a bowl and keep it nearby.

Remove the handle of the faucet by removing the screws holding it in place. Most screws are hidden under some sort of decorative element, so look for a little cap to pry off with a screwdriver.

From there, repair the leak according to what kind of faucet you're dealing with.

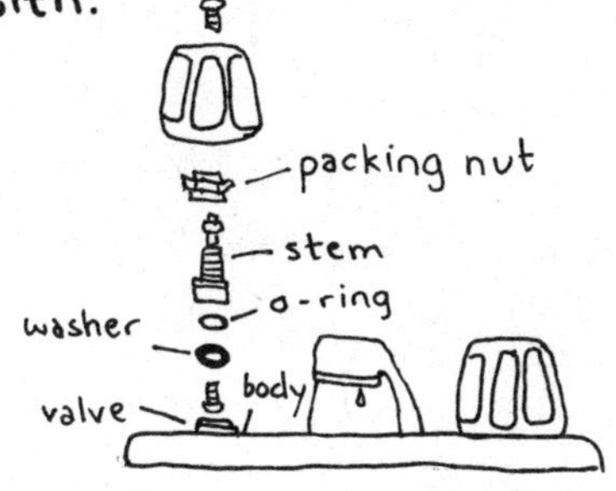

Compression Faucets

Step 1: Remove the large packing nut and pull the stem straight up out of the faucet body.

Step 2: Remove the screw holding the washer onto the assembly. Remove the washer and pull the stem out to remove the O-ring as well.

Step 3: Dunk the parts in vinegar and scrub them with a scouring pad to remove mineral buildup. Replace the washer and O-ring and reassemble the stem.

Step 4: Place everything from the faucet back into the faucet in the order you took it out. Replace the packing nut, tighten it, and pop the handle on top.

Replace the handle holding the handle on the faucet and press the cap on top of it. Turn on the water and test out your fancy new drip-free faucet.

Rotating Ball Faucets

handle
cap
spout
cam ball assembly
seals
springs
o-rings
body

Replacement parts for this type of faucet come in kits that include special tools you need for repairs.

Step 1: Use an Allen wrench to loosen the handle screws and remove the handle. Loosen the adjusting ring with the special tool from the repair kit.

Step 2: Use pliers to unscrew the cap covering the cam ball. Lift out the ball and remove the spout as well.

Step 3: Look inside the faucet body and see if you can spot the rubber seals. Remove each seal with the tip of a screwdriver. Repeat with the little springs under the seals.

Step 4: Pry or cut the old O-rings from around the faucet body. Lube the faucet and roll new O-rings down into place. Replace the spout.

Step 5: Use your fingers to press new springs and seals into the faucet body. Insert the ball on top, fitting the tab in the ball into the slot in the faucet body.

Step 6: Screw the cap on top of the cam ball, add the handle and re-tighten the screw set.

Cartridge Faucets

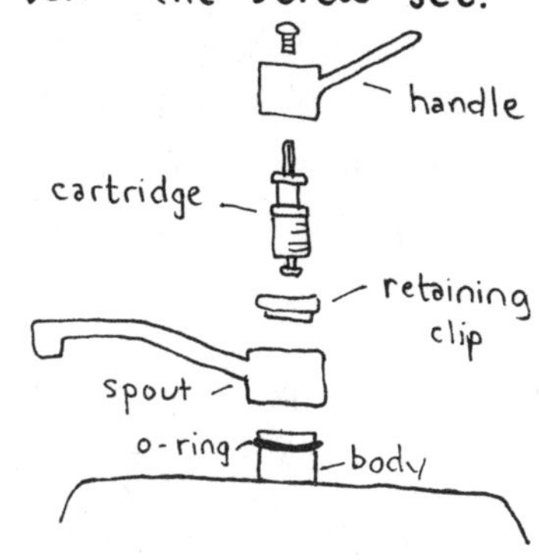

Instead of replacing a washer or seal, cartridge faucets require you to replace the whole cartridge. You might want to pull the cartridge out first and take it with you to the hardware store.

Step 1: Use a screwdriver to remove the handle screw. Lift off the handle.

Step 2: Remove the retaining clip from the faucet body using needle-nose pliers. Pull the cartridge straight up from the faucet to remove it.

Step 3: Remove the spout and replace the O-rings if necessary (see Rotating Ball Faucets).

Step 4: Replace the spout, pop a new cartridge into the faucet (face it the same way as the old cartridge), and fit the retainer clip around it.

Step 5: Replace the handle and handle screw, and turn the water back on.

Disc Faucets

Like rotating ball faucets, leaky disc faucets are usually the result of worn-out seals. Replacement kits will include the seals and any other parts you may need.

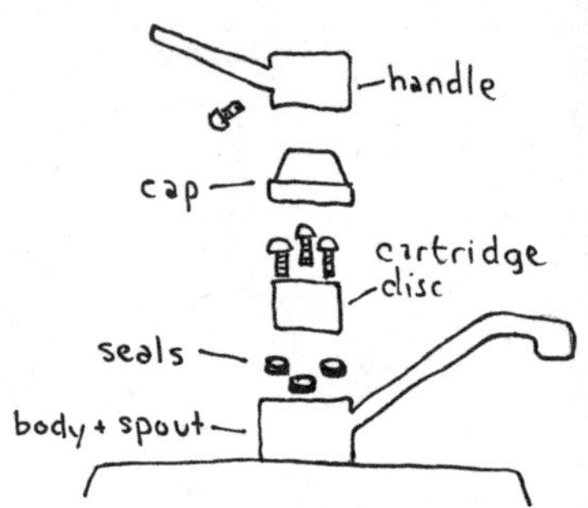

Step 1: Use a screwdriver to remove the handle and the cap that covers the cartridge.

Step 2: The cartridge disc is held in place with a few small screws. Loosen these and pull the disc straight up out of the faucet.

Step 3: Flip the cartridge disc over and check out the seals on its bottom. Pull out any worn or cracked seals. Give the cartridge a nice scrub with vinegar.

Step 4: Press in new seals with your fingers. Turn the disc right side up and pop it back in the faucet, making sure to align the seals with the holes in the faucet body.

Step 5: Secure the disc screws, screw the cap back on, and replace the handle. Turn on the water. Voila!

TOILETS

Here's a theory: Toilets are intimidating. It's weird to think of something so humble and literally full of crap as scary, but how else do you explain the kneejerk reaction to call the plumber when we hear so much as a gurgle? So many of us just don't want to handle toilet repair (pun intended), and that's silly. The fear ends now!

Anatomy of a Toilet

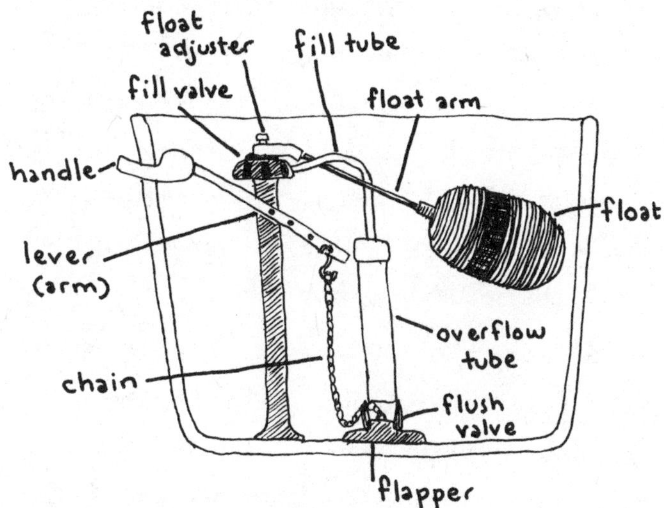

Fixing a Loose Toilet Handle

Let's get this toilet party started, eh? First up, what to do about that worrysome jiggle.

Step 1: Find the shut-off valve behind the toilet and turn the water off. If there isn't a shut-off valve, go ahead and turn off the main water supply. Flush the toilet once or twice to lower the level of water in the toilet tank.

Step 2: Carefully remove the lid of the tank and set it aside. Inside the tank, you'll see the stem of the handle, a flushing lever with a chain attached, and a nut joining the two.

For a jiggly handle, your first course of action is to tighten the handle nut. (These particular nuts are reverse-thread, so remember that when you're tightening it.) Grab a wrench and give the nut a couple of good turns counterclockwise. If the nut's not loose after all, move your attention down to the flushing lever.

Step 3: Take the chain off the lever and shorten it by re-hooking it to the lever a little further down. Leave some slack in the chain, though! Turn the water back on and flush to see if that fixes the problem.

Step 4: Still jiggling? Ugh! Okay, one more idea. Next to the lever you should see a wire and float ball coming out from the flush valve. Use your hands to bend that wire and lift the float ball up a little. That should help tighten some of the slack in the handle. Turn on the water (if it's not on already) and flush to see if that helped.

Replacing a Toilet Handle

If fiddling with the nut, chain, and float doesn't fix your handle problem, it's okay. Handles are easy enough to replace. Just make sure you know what size handle and lever you have and shop for one that fits. (Tip: If the lever's just a little too long, you can use a hacksaw to shorten it before you do the installation.)

Step 1: If you haven't already, shut off the water to the toilet and remove the toilet tank lid.

Step 2: Remove the chain from the lever.

Step 3: Use a wrench to take off the nut inside the tank, and remove the handle and lever.

If your toilet has a float cup, just squeeze the clip on the side with your thumb and forefinger and inch the cup down a little.

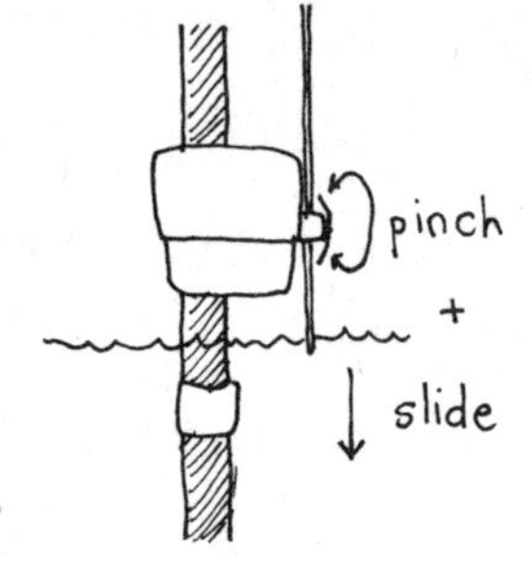

Once adjustments have been made, flush and make sure the water level is below the overflow tube but not so low that the bowl is too empty.

Observation: Water level's fine, and when you push down on the flapper with a stick, the trickling noises stop.

Problem: Your flapper's shot. It might just be gunked up with mineral residue, or it might be worn out. Either way, you need to get it out of the tank.

To replace a flapper, turn off the water, flush to empty the tank, and take the chain off the hook. Unhook the flapper from the bottom of the overflow tube and slide it up the tube to remove it.

If your flapper is gunky, clean it thoroughly. Then slide either the clean flapper or a new one down into position at the base of the overflow tube. Make sure the flapper fits tightly into the bottom of the tank. Rehook the chain and turn the water back on.

Replacing a Toilet's Wax Ring

If you've ever lived somewhere with a bathroom that just *stank*, no matter what you did, you've already learned a lesson about the importance of a toilet's wax ring. Squished between the porcelain and the floor, the ring keeps the toilet stable and prevents water (and smells) from leaking out.

If you notice water coming from the base of your toilet, consistent sewer-y odors, or if the toilet rocks while you're on it, replace the ring pronto.

Equipment:

* plunger
* rags
* wrench
* putty knife
* new wax ring
* a helper

Step 1: Turn off the water supply going to the toilet, flush a few times to make sure all the water is out of the tank, and use a plunger to push any remaining bowl water into the pipes below. Have a few rags handy to clean up any spills.

Step 2: Use a wrench to remove the nut connecting the toilet to the water supply line.

Step 3: Remove the plastic caps covering the nuts that hold down the base of the toilet. Remove the nuts as well.

Step 4: Pick up that toilet! Yep. You should get a helper. Turn the toilet over and rest it, upside down, on plenty of rags or newspaper.

Step 5: Hey, guess what? That old wax seal probably looks disgusting. Use a putty knife to scrape away as much nasty wax as you can from the bottom of the toilet and the flange (the area on the floor around the pipe).

Step 6: Take your nice, new, clean wax ring and place it, wax side down, onto the bottom of the toilet. Press the ring a little so that it won't fall off when you turn the toilet back over.

Step 7: Pick up the toilet again (oy), turn it over, and carefully place it back on top of the flange. Go slow and make sure the bolts on the floor align with the holes in the base of the toilet.

Step 8: Time for a rest! Sit on the toilet (KEEP YOUR PANTS ON) and rock around a little. Your weight will compress the new wax ring and help it squeeze into all the nooks and crannies it needs to.

Step 9: Replace the nuts on the toilet's base, tightening each nut a little at a time. (Careful you don't tighten too much; it could crack the porcelain.) Reconnect the water supply and tighten that nut as well.

Step 10: Double-check all your nuts and water connections, and if they're secure, turn the water back on.

Step 11: Mop your floor.

Home Repair Resources

Dare to Repair: A Do-It-Herself Guide to Fixing (Almost) Anything in the Home
by Julie Sussman & Stephanie Glakas-Tenet
New York: Harper Collins, 2002

This Old House Essential Home Repair: A Seasonal Guide to Maintaining Your Home
New York: This Old House Books, 1999

Yankee Magazine's Make It Last: Over 1,000 Ingenious Ways to Extend the Life of Everything You Own
by Earl Proulx
Emmaus, PA: Yankee Books, 1996

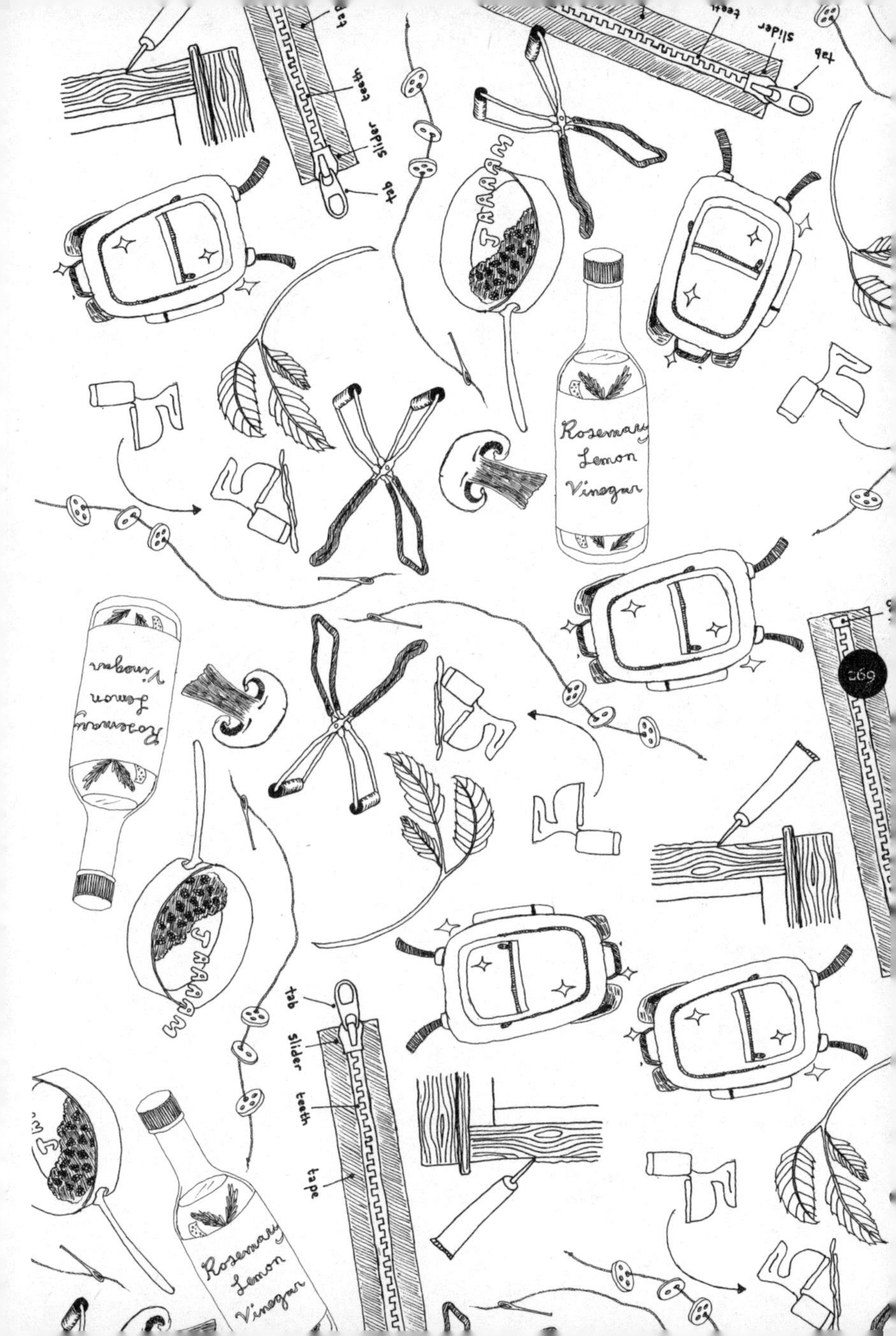
tab
slider
teeth
tape
Rosemary
Lemon
Vinegar
TAAAAM

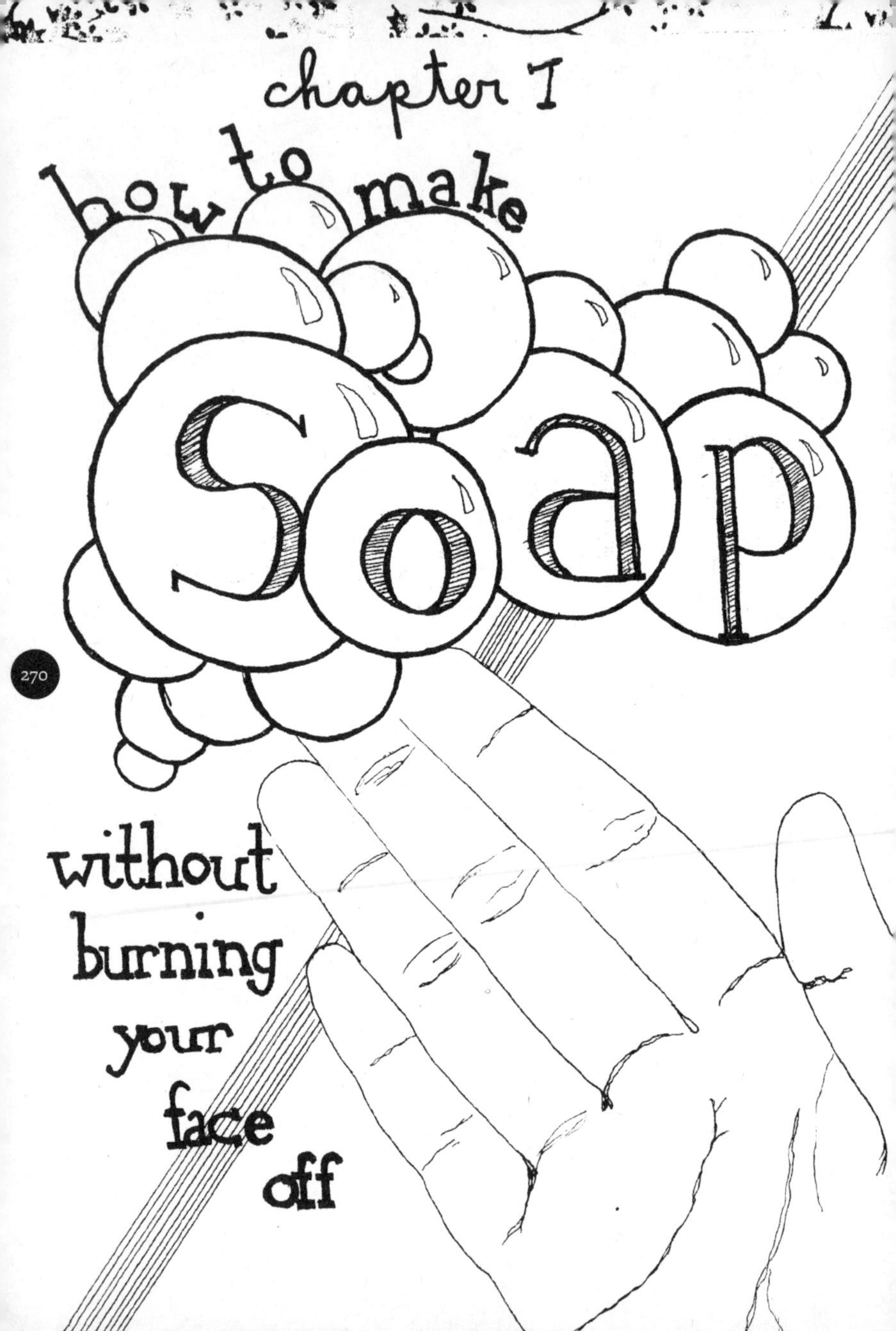
chapter 7
how to make
Soap
without
burning
your
face
off

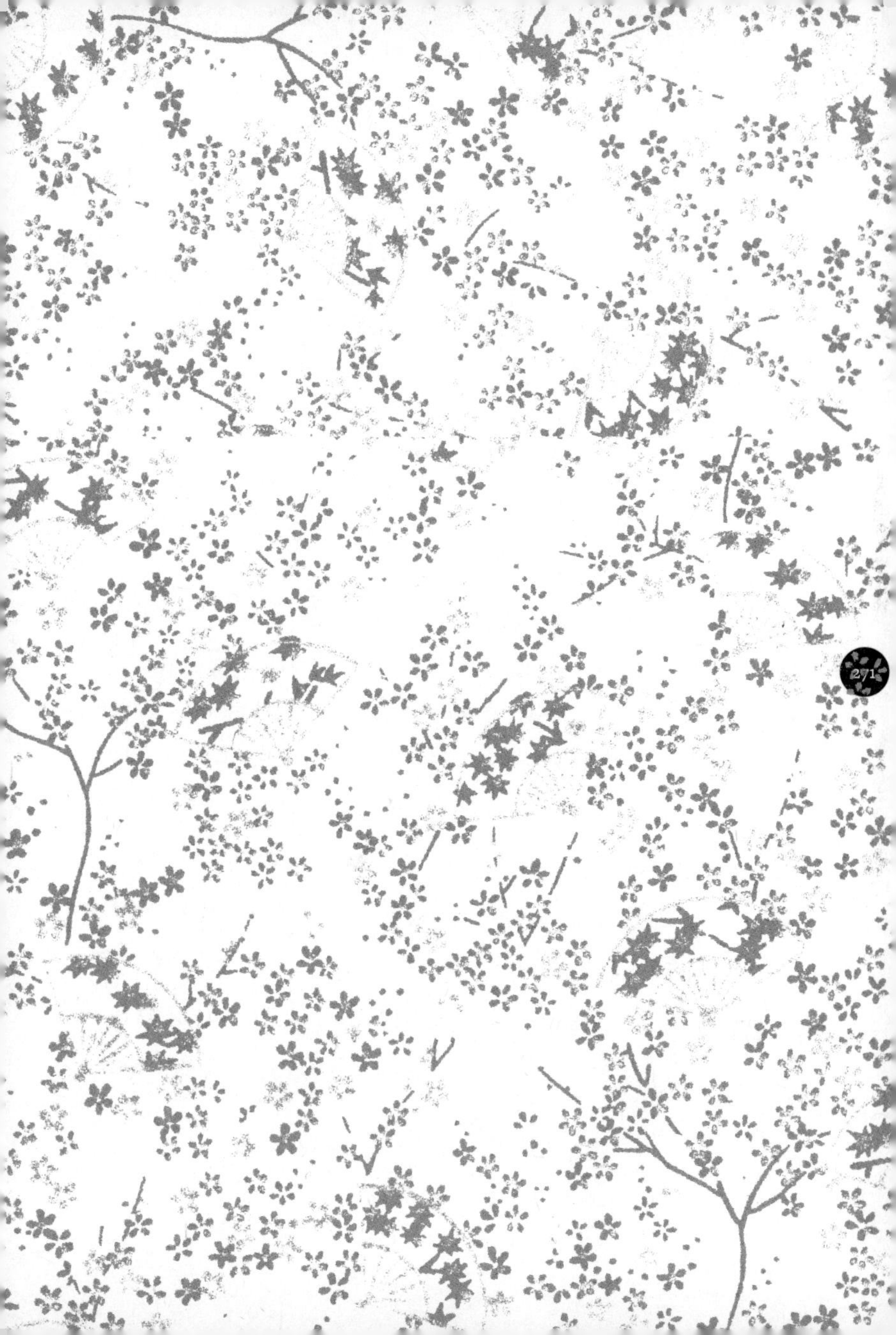

PLEASE READ

The process detailed in this zine requires a lot of care and attention. Some of the substances used to make soap are potentially very dangerous. Neither I nor the good folks at Microcosm can be responsible for you if you hurt yourself, someone else, or otherwise get into trouble. Please read all the instructions before you begin. Don't cut corners, especially with safety precautions — even if you've made soap before. Above all, take care of yourselves, and your friends, and have fun!

First, a history lesson...

Soap in its most basic form is created by combining some form of fat with a strong alkaline substance, a process called saponification. There are many theories about how humans got a handle on saponification. A popular legend is that soap was discovered in ancient Rome, on a mountain called Sapo. Maybe you've heard this? According to the story, when the fat from sacrificed animals ran down the side of the mountain to a river below, it mixed with the ashes from the burnt offerings and a crude soap formed in the river water. Thus the good people of Sapo were able to do their laundry.

While this story is really fun and creepy, it's not true. Nobody can find anything resembing Mount Sapo, and no one in Rome wrote about the phenomenon, either. Sorry, kids! I know how much you liked that gross story.* In reality, soap (in its modern formulation) has been in use all over the world since the early centuries of the Common Era. For most of that time, soap was made on a very small scale, and mostly used for laundry and household cleaning, as it was usually too harsh for bathing. Increasing awareness of hygiene and its ability to curb the spread of disease led to the large-scale industrial manufacturing of soap in the late 18th century. By the time the Industrial Revolution rolled (and in some places is still rolling) around, it was pretty normal to buy things instead of making them, and hand-made soap became more of a rarity. It's funny, then, that today "artisinal" soaps are a sort of fancy treat for people. Full circle!

*As an aside, can we please stop pretending that Romans invented everything? Give it a rest already.

About lye...

A few years ago I wrote a zine about nontoxic housecleaning. I didn't include any soap recipes in the zine because lye is quite poisonous and demands serious respect. It's kind of opposite of nontoxic. We all saw that movie. But I'm ready to talk about lye now, so here we go:

Lye is the lay term for a caustic alkaline compound, sodium hydroxide (NaOH). It is usually, though not always, the primary chemical used in making soap (potassium hydroxide is used to make liquid soap). Lye can be pretty intimidating for beginners, but alas, you can't make soap bars without it. Fortunately, it only takes a few precautions to keep things from getting hairy.

• Always buy 100% lye, and not drain cleaner, which usually consists of lye + a lot of other crap. You can find it at hardware stores - but bring your ID, some places restrict the sale of lye because it's used in meth production.

• When lye and water meet, they get very hot very quickly. You should know this, and you should know that the combination creates fumes you don't want to breathe.. Always work in a very well-ventilated area. It's best if you can mix your lye and water outdoors; second best is to open a couple windows and point a fan out of one of them.

• Keep kids and animals out of your soapmaking area, including your lye-mixing area.

• Protect yourself by wearing safety goggles and thick rubber gloves. Long sleeves and close-toed shoes are also a good idea.

• Lastly, if lye gets on your skin, you can neutralize it by dousing your skin with vinegar. Keep a big bottle of vinegar around for this purpose.

Although it's possible to create soap using a single fat, most handmade soaps use a combination of oils. Each fat you'll encounter has a different assortment of fatty acids. Different fatty acids contribute to a soap's hardness, durability, lather, and moisturizing ability. The recipes in this zine will only use vegetable fats, but most commercial soaps are made with tallow. Tallow is rendered cow's fat. It's dirt cheap and creates a nice bar of soap, but there are so many other options to explore. The best soap has a good balance of hardening, lathering, and cleansing oils (see the handy chart to see which oils do what).

Hardening	Lathering	Moisturizing
palm *	coconut	olive
shea butter	castor	canola
jojoba	palm kernel*	soybean
beeswax	cottonseed (aka vegetable shortening - use organic, cotton plants are heavily sprayed)	sunflower
cocoa butter		rice bran
(lard + tallow)		safflower

SUPERFATS!
apricot kernel
sweet almond
avocado
kukui nut
wheatgerm

SUPERFATTING happens when there is a little more oil than lye in your soap. The extra oil ends up on your skin instead of getting saponified. Superfatting does two things:

① It makes your soap more lovely and moisturizing

② It ensures that your soap is mild enough. If there's too much lye in your soap it can be caustic; adding more oil gives you some wiggle room. In some books it might be referred to as "lye discounting."

You can use whatever oil you want for superfatting, including the ones you're already using in the recipe. But since you only need a little bit, why not try something nice?

The Process!

FIRST YOU NEED:

- a stockpot with handles (steel, enamel, or pyrex)
- a pyrex or heat-resistant plastic pitcher
- a glass mason jar
- a big mixing bowl
- two easy-to-read metal thermometers
- a scale
- two spoons (one plastic, one wooden)
- rubber gloves and goggles
- molds for the soap (see step 6)
- a towel or blanket
- emergency vinegar

all your oils, lye, additives, etc. See Recipes section!

1) Like most things, soapmaking goes smoothest if you have your shit together: measure all your ingredients beforehand and have your materials handy. Line your work area with newspapers and put on your gloves and goggles.

2) Take your pitcher, mason jar, lye and water to a well-ventilated area, outside if possible. Measure water into the pitcher and lye into the jar. Use a scale and measure by weight. Place both on a steady surface and attach a thermometer to the pitcher.

6) Annnd keep stirring! FOREVER. Here's the thing about soap: you have to stir it for a really long time, anywhere from 45 minutes to 3 hours. It's totally bearable if you have a few friends to help you. Another option, if you have a little money, is to buy a stick blender – more on that coming pages. In either case what you're looking for is soap thick enough to leave a trace behind when you run your spoon through it. This is appropriately called the trace stage.

5) When lye has reached the same temperature as oil, add the lye mixture to the pot in a slow stream whilst stirring diligently. Have someone else put the lye pitcher in a safe place + keep stirring...

4) Weigh your fats in the plastic bowl, add them to the pot, and heat them to 110°. Watch the temperature closely. If you're using solid fats, weigh them in the pot and melt them before adding the liquid fat.

3) Add the lye to the water a little at a time and stir it with the wooden spoon until it's dissolved. Watch out – the water will get very hot, at least 200°. ALWAYS add lye to water, not the other way around. If you pour water on a heap of lye it will cause a teensy explosion. Put the pitcher in a safe place and let it cool to 110 degrees.

7) When that sweet, sweet trace has been acheived, you can add your essential oils, scrubby bits, glitter, etc. Add fragrances first, exfoliants and textural bits second, and colorants last. Stir until everything is well blended but not too thick to pour.

8) Line your mold if it's not lined already. Use parchment paper and tape it down. A narrow wooden box is the best mold, especially if it has a lid. Another good option is a semi-flexible plastic container, which you can oil lightly instead of lining. Pour your soap into the mold and smooth the top with a spatula. Pick up the mold and drop it a couple of times to dislodge any air bubbles.

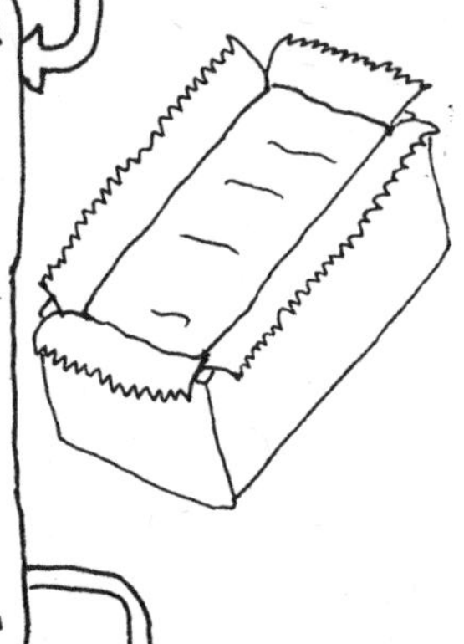

9.) Time to put your soap to bed for a day or two. Put a lid on your mold, wrap the whole thing in a towel or blanket, and put it in a warm place. Leave it alone for 24 hours so it can cure. In the meantime leave your gloves on while you wash your equipment with hot, soapy water.*

After your soap has rested you can unmold it and cut it into bars; use a knife or a length of wire. Lay the bars out on a rack and let them dry out for a few weeks. Drying the soap will make it gentler and longer-lasting. If you try to use it right after you make it your soap will just melt in the shower.

If you really can't resist, at least wait a few days.

*But not your wooden lye spoon. It's gone forever. Sorry!

Special Tricks

• Using colorants: there are a few different tricks for coloring soap. Wax crayons actually work pretty well, but only certain colors of crayon. Cerulean is the best one to use, but yellow, orange, black and white work well too. Add up to a teaspoon of a spice to make nice warm, autumnal colors: turmeric makes a deep gOld; paprika makes peach; cocoa powder makes a warm brown. The easiest way to make green soap is to start your batch with herb-infused oils. Comfrey leaf in particular is deep green and has skin-healing properties.

• Using additives: adding scrubby stuff like oatmeal or cornmeal to your soap invigorates your skin and makes your recipes more unique. Start with a cup of your chosen additive and add more if you need it. Plant bits like lavender buds and calendula petals are nice too, although they won't retain their colors through the soaping process. Sea salt and green clay are good additives for oily skin.

• Using a stick blender will bring your soap to trace very quickly, but you have to use it carefully. When you're adding your lye to your oils, use the blender as a spoon instead of turning it on. As soon as all the lye has been added you can start turning the blender on for five seconds at a time, stirring in between pUlses. Your batch will thicken in just a few minutes, but resist the temptation to keep the blender humming - you don't want your soap to get too thick before you add your additives and scents in. If it does, you'll be stuck with boring soap, and it will be your own fault.

• Sometimes you might unmold your soap to find that a white layer of "ash" has formed on top. This is not a big deal: just cut or scrape it off and proceed!

START HERE →
OR HERE
↓

Basic Soap Recipe #1 (Makes 5 pounds, or 48 bars!)

This recipe contains coconut oil for lather, olive oil for its emollient properties, and vegetable shortening to harden the bar. I added some cocoa butter to superfat the soap.

24 oz coconut oil
28 oz olive oil
24 oz shortening
4 oz cocoa butter
30.4 oz water
11.4 oz lye crystals
½ - 1 oz essential oil*

Basic Soap Recipe #2

(Makes 5 lbs, or 48 bars)

This recipe improves on recipe #1 with the addition of castor oil (for creamy lather) and canola and sunflower oils (for moisture).

20 oz olive oil
20 oz coconut oil
20 oz shortening
8 oz canola oil
8 oz sunflower oil
4 oz castor oil
21.7 oz water
11.2 oz lye crystals
½ - 1 oz essential oil*

* If you're using fragrance oil instead of essential oil, you can use a little more in your recipe.

Healing Soap for dry skin, eczema, upset skin

Use Recipe #2. A few days before you start, add 1 cup each comfrey leaf and calendula petals to the olive oil you're using. Strain all the solid bits out of the oil before you make soap. Use orange blossom or lavender oil (or both!) for fragrance.

Scrubby Soap for dirty hands

Use Recipe #1. After you hit the trace stage, add ½ cup each cornmeal and oatmeal to your soap. Use a citrus oil like lemon or bergamot for fragrance. If you want to, add a tea spoon or more of turmeric for color.

Oatmeal Soap for itchy skin

Use Recipe #2. Replace the water in the recipe with rose petal tea. Use chamomile and rose oils for fragrance (don't use chamomile if you are allergic to ragweed). Add up to a cup of coarsely ground oatmeal.

Femme Soap

Use Recipe #1. Replace the water in the recipe with rose petal or jasmine flower tea, or use flower-infused oils. Add some glitter during the additive stage and color with 1 teaspoon of paprika for a nice peachy color. For scent, use rose*, jasmine, rose geranium, neroli, or ylang-ylang essential oil.

Good Morning Soap

Use either recipe. Use peppermint tea instead of water. After trace stage, add ½ c each sea salt and sand or pumice powder. Make sure to use clean, fine sand. Add basil and peppermint oils for scent.

Sleepy Soap

Use either recipe. After trace stage, add up to a cup of lavender flowers. Use chamomile and rosemary oils for scent + soothing properties.

Swirly Soap

If monochromatic soap is too boring for you, add some visual interest with a nice swirly pattern. If you've ever tempered an egg-based sauce, it's basically the same process. If this interests you, read on:

When it comes time to add colorant, scoop out about a cup's worth of soap. Add your colorant to this little bit, mix it well, and then drizzle the colored soap back into the pot. Hold the cup a few inches from the bowl so you don't get too much in one place. Swirl the soap gently with a rubber spatula to achieve desired marbling.

* use rose perfume oil, rose essential oil is crazy expensive

MORE BY RALEIGH BRIGGS FROM www.MICROCOSM.PUB

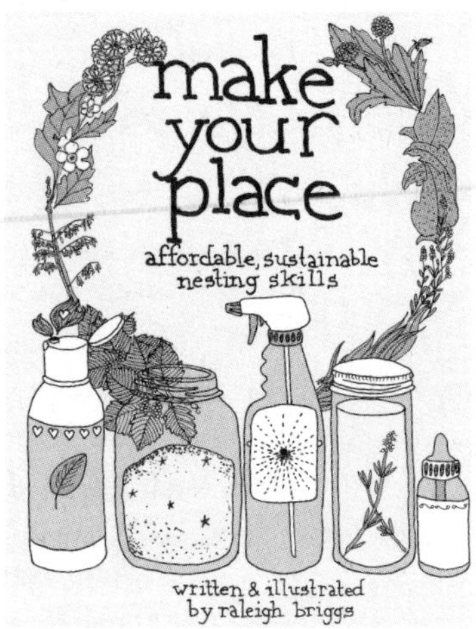

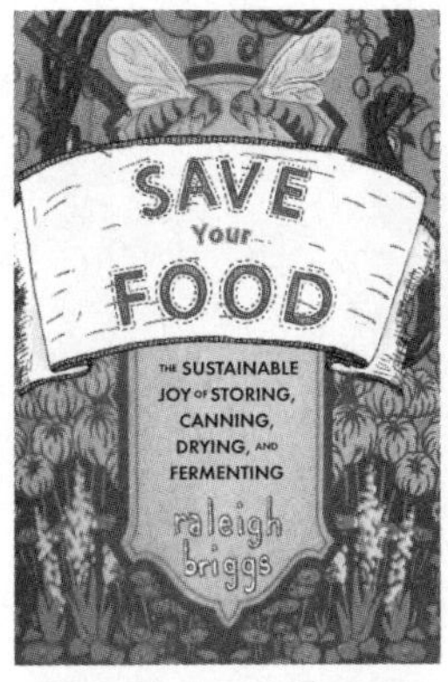
SAVE
Your
FOOD
THE SUSTAINABLE JOY OF STORING, CANNING, DRYING, AND FERMENTING
raleigh briggs

FIX
Your
HOME
THE SUSTAINABLE ART OF PATCHING, PLUMBING, AND REPAIRING
raleigh briggs

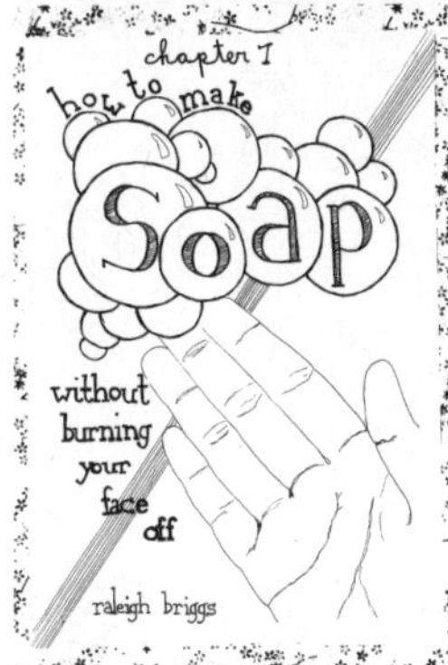
chapter 7
how to make
Soap
without burning your face off
raleigh briggs

herbal first aid
(assembling a natural first aid kit)
(ARNICA)

avoid dangerous chemicals!
so clean!
so damn nice & clean
nontoxic housecleaning

CREATE THE LIFE AND WORLD THAT YOU WANT TO LIVE IN AT MICROCOSM.PUB

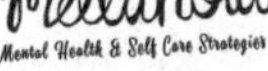

METTANOIA
VOLUME TWO
Mental Health & Self Care Strategies

Mettanoia
Mental Health & Self Care Strategies

Mettanoia
(volume 4)
Mental Health & Self Care Strategies

METTANOIA
VOLUME SEVEN
Mental Health & Self Care Strategies

Find release from your cares, have a good time.

SUBSCRIBE!

For as little as $15/month, you can support a small, independent publisher and get every book that we publish—delivered to your doorstep!

www.Microcosm.Pub/BFF

MORE SUSTAINABLE LIFESTYLES FROM MICROCOSM.PUB

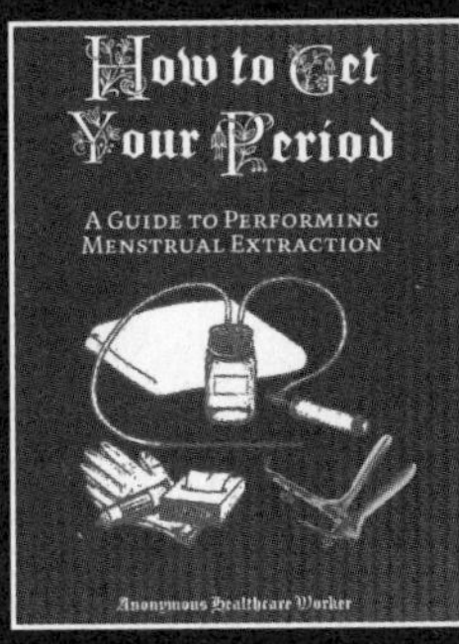

SUBSCRIBE!

For as little as $15/month, you can support a small, independent publisher and get every book that we publish—delivered to your doorstep!

www.Microcosm.Pub/BFF

MORE HOUSE AND HOME REVOLUTION FROM MICROCOSM.PUB

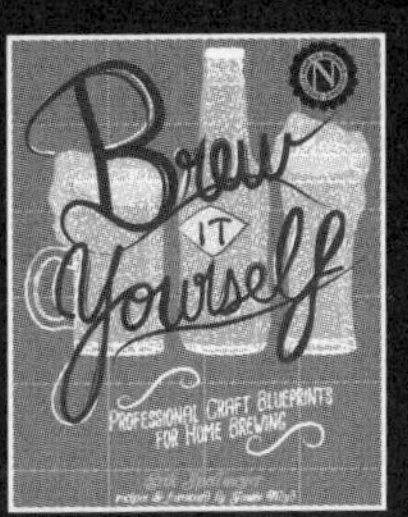

Rosemary
Lemon
Vinegar
THAAARM
stop
tape
teeth
slider
tab